Puppet 5 Essentials

Third Edition

A fast-paced guide to automating your infrastructure

Martin Alfke

Felix Frank

BIRMINGHAM - MUMBAI

Puppet 5 Essentials

Third Edition

First published: November 2014

Second edition: December 2015

Third edition: September 2017

Production reference: 1080917

Published by Packt Publishing Ltd.
Livery Place
35 Livery Street
Birmingham
B3 2PB, UK.
ISBN 978-1-78728-471-5

www.packtpub.com

Credits

Authors
Martin Alfke
Felix Frank

Reviewer
Thomas Dao

Commissioning Editor
Pratik Shah

Acquisition Editor
Chandan Kumar

Content Development Editor
Mamata Walkar

Technical Editor
Varsha Shivhare

Copy Editor
Safis Editing

Project Coordinator
Kinjal Bari

Proofreader
Safis Editing

Indexer
Pratik Shirodkar

Graphics
Kirk D'Penha

Production Coordinator
Shantanu Zagade

About the Authors

Martin Alfke is the co-founder and CEO of example42 GmbH. He has been a Puppet and automation enthusiast since 2007 and has delivered official Puppet training in Germany since 2011. In the past, he would have said that he is a system administrator. Nowadays, he prefers the term infrastructure engineer. The big difference is that system administrators ssh into systems, whereas infrastructure engineers fix their automation. With example42 GmbH, Martin supports Puppet Inc as a Puppet service delivery partner. He likes giving talks and workshops at conferences around the globe.

Felix Frank has used and programmed computers for most of his life. During and after working on his computer science diploma, he gained experience on the job as a systems administrator, server operator, and open source software developer. He spent six years of his eleven year career as a Puppet power user. In parallel, he spent about two years intensifying his studies through ongoing source code contributions and active participation in several conferences.

About the Reviewer

Thomas Dao has worn many hats in IT, from Unix administration, build/release engineering, DevOps engineering, Android development, and now, dad to his bundle of joy, Carina. He also enjoys being an organizer of the Eastside Android Developers GDG meetup group. He can be reached at tom@tomseattle.com.

www.PacktPub.com

For support files and downloads related to your book, please visit www.PacktPub.com.

Did you know that Packt offers eBook versions of every book published, with PDF and ePub files available? You can upgrade to the eBook version at www.PacktPub.com and as a print book customer, you are entitled to a discount on the eBook copy. Get in touch with us at service@packtpub.com for more details.

At www.PacktPub.com, you can also read a collection of free technical articles, sign up for a range of free newsletters and receive exclusive discounts and offers on Packt books and eBooks.

https://www.packtpub.com/mapt

Get the most in-demand software skills with Mapt. Mapt gives you full access to all Packt books and video courses, as well as industry-leading tools to help you plan your personal development and advance your career.

Why subscribe?

- Fully searchable across every book published by Packt
- Copy and paste, print, and bookmark content
- On demand and accessible via a web browser

Customer Feedback

Thanks for purchasing this Packt book. At Packt, quality is at the heart of our editorial process. To help us improve, please leave us an honest review on this book's Amazon page at https://www.amazon.com/dp/1787284719.

If you'd like to join our team of regular reviewers, you can e-mail us at customerreviews@packtpub.com. We award our regular reviewers with free eBooks and videos in exchange for their valuable feedback. Help us be relentless in improving our products!

Table of Contents

Preface

Puppet is a configuration management tool that allows you to automate all your IT configurations, giving you control over what you do with each Puppet agent in a network, and when and how you do it. In this age of digital delivery and ubiquitous internet presence, it's becoming increasingly important to implement scalable and portable solutions, not only in terms of software but also the system that runs it.

This book aims to impart knowledge required to tap into not only the basics of Puppet, but also its core. The very basic ideas and principles of Puppet-based designs are explored and explained in this book. A sophisticated tool is presented to enable efficient and productive use.

What this book covers

Chapter 1, *Writing Your First Manifests*, explains Puppet declarative configuration management based on resources and how to implement them.

Chapter 2, *Puppet Server and Agents*, covers installation and configuration of Puppet Server, and how to comment agents to the server.

Chapter 3, *A Peek into the Ruby Part of Puppet - Facts, Types, and Providers*, explains the underlying functions of Facter and its facts, types, and providers in Puppet.

Chapter 4, *Combining Resources in Classes and Defined Types*, covers self-defined resources that allow you to simplify a repetitive code.

Chapter 5, *Combining Classes, Configuration Files, and Extensions into Modules*, explains the concepts of Puppet environments and node classification.

Chapter 6, *The Puppet Beginners Advanced Parts*, covers the Puppet features that offer readability, flexibility, and improvements such as EPP templates, virtual and exported resources, and resource defaults.

Chapter 7, *New Features from Puppet 4 and 5*, explains the concept of Puppet environments and node classification.

Chapter 8, *Separation of Code and Data with Hiera*, covers a Puppet way of separating code and data, so data can be managed.

Chapter 9, *Puppet Roles and Profiles*, provides a workflow that allows separate upgrades of upstream modules and local Puppet implementations.

What you need for this book

You need Debian 8+ or Ubuntu 14+, and physical/virtual x86.

Who this book is for

This book is meant for an experienced IT professionals and new Puppet users. This book will provide you with all you need to know to go from installation to advanced automation. Get a rapid introduction to the essential topics and learn how to build best practices for advanced automation with Puppet.

Conventions

In this book, you will find a number of text styles that distinguish between different kinds of information. Here are some examples of these styles and an explanation of their meaning.

Code words in text, database table names, folder names, filenames, file extensions, pathnames, dummy URLs, user input, and Twitter handles are shown as follows: "The file resource type will return `mtime` and `ctime`."

A block of code is set as follows:

```
node 'agent' {
    $packages = [ 'apache2', 'libapache2-mod-php5', 'libapache2-mod-
passenger', ]
    package { $packages:
      ensure => 'installed',
      before => Service['apache2'],
    }
    service { 'apache2':
      ensure => 'running',
      enable => true,
    }
}
```

When we wish to draw your attention to a particular part of a code block, the relevant lines or items are set in bold:

```
service { 'puppet': enable => false }
cron { 'puppet-agent-run':
  user      => 'root',
  command =>
    'puppet agent --no-daemonize --onetime --
    logdest=syslog',
  minute => fqdn_rand(60),
  hour    => absent,
}
```

Any command-line input or output is written as follows:

```
puppet:///modules/ntp/ntp.conf
puppet:///modules/my_app/opt/scripts/find_my_app.sh
```

New terms and **important words** are shown in bold. Words that you see on the screen, for example, in menus or dialog boxes, appear in the text like this: "If you are looking for a module that will enhance your agents through additional resource types and providers, look for the **Types** tab on the module details page. "

Warnings or important notes appear like this.

Tips and tricks appear like this.

Reader feedback

Feedback from our readers is always welcome. Let us know what you think about this book-what you liked or disliked. Reader feedback is important for us as it helps us develop titles that you will really get the most out of. To send us general feedback, simply email feedback@packtpub.com, and mention the book's title in the subject of your message. If there is a topic that you have expertise in and you are interested in either writing or contributing to a book, see our author guide at www.packtpub.com/authors.

Customer support

Now that you are the proud owner of a Packt book, we have a number of things to help you to get the most from your purchase.

Downloading the example code

You can download the example code files for this book from your account at `http://www.packtpub.com`. If you purchased this book elsewhere, you can visit `http://www.packtpub.com/support` and register to have the files emailed directly to you. You can download the code files by following these steps:

1. Log in or register to our website using your email address and password.
2. Hover the mouse pointer on the **SUPPORT** tab at the top.
3. Click on **Code Downloads & Errata**.
4. Enter the name of the book in the **Search** box.
5. Select the book for which you're looking to download the code files.
6. Choose from the drop-down menu where you purchased this book from.
7. Click on **Code Download**.

Once the file is downloaded, please make sure that you unzip or extract the folder using the latest version of:

- WinRAR / 7-Zip for Windows
- Zipeg / iZip / UnRarX for Mac
- 7-Zip / PeaZip for Linux

The code bundle for the book is also hosted on GitHub at `https://github.com/PacktPublishing/Puppet-Essentials-Third-Edition`. We also have other code bundles from our rich catalog of books and videos available at `https://github.com/PacktPublishing/`. Check them out!

Downloading the color images of this book

We also provide you with a PDF file that has color images of the screenshots/diagrams used in this book. The color images will help you better understand the changes in the output. You can download this file from `http://www.packtpub.com/sites/default/files/downloads/PuppetEssentialsThirdEdition_ColorImages.pdf`.

Errata

Although we have taken every care to ensure the accuracy of our content, mistakes do happen. If you find a mistake in one of our books-maybe a mistake in the text or the code-we would be grateful if you could report this to us. By doing so, you can save other readers from frustration and help us improve subsequent versions of this book. If you find any errata, please report them by visiting http://www.packtpub.com/submit-errata, selecting your book, clicking on the **Errata Submission Form** link, and entering the details of your errata. Once your errata are verified, your submission will be accepted and the errata will be uploaded to our website or added to any list of existing errata under the Errata section of that title. To view the previously submitted errata, go to https://www.packtpub.com/books/content/support and enter the name of the book in the search field. The required information will appear under the **Errata** section.

Piracy

Piracy of copyrighted material on the internet is an ongoing problem across all media. At Packt, we take the protection of our copyright and licenses very seriously. If you come across any illegal copies of our works in any form on the internet, please provide us with the location address or website name immediately so that we can pursue a remedy. Please contact us at copyright@packtpub.com with a link to the suspected pirated material. We appreciate your help in protecting our authors and our ability to bring you valuable content.

Questions

If you have a problem with any aspect of this book, you can contact us at questions@packtpub.com, and we will do our best to address the problem.

1
Writing Your First Manifests

Configuration management has become essential to the IT world. Faster development using agile methods has a huge impact on IT operations that need to keep pace with the faster deployment of systems. Server operations in general are hardly even feasible without a robust management infrastructure. Among the available tools, Puppet has established itself as one of the most popular and widespread solutions. Originally written by Luke Kanies, the tool is now distributed under the terms of Apache License 2.0 and maintained by Luke's company, Puppet Inc. It boasts a large and bustling community, rich APIs for plugins and supporting tools, outstanding online documentation, and a great security model based on SSL authentication.

Like all configuration management systems, Puppet allows you to maintain a central repository of infrastructure definitions, along with a toolchain to enforce the desired state on the systems under management. The whole feature set is quite impressive. This book will guide you through some steps to quickly grasp the most important aspects and principles of Puppet.

In this chapter, we will cover the following topics:

- Getting started
- Introducing resources, parameters, and properties
- Interpreting the output of the `puppet apply` command
- Using variables
- Adding control structures in manifests
- Controlling the order of execution
- Implementing resource interaction
- Examining Puppet core resource types

Getting started

Installing Puppet is easy. On large Linux distributions, you can just install the Puppet package via `apt-get` or `yum`.

The installation of Puppet can be done in the following ways:

- From default operating system repositories
- From Puppet Inc

The former way is generally simpler. `Chapter 2`, *Puppet Server and Agents*, provides simple instructions to install the Puppet Inc packages. A platform-independent way to install Puppet is to get the `puppet` Ruby gem. This is fine for testing and managing single systems, but it is not recommended for production use.

After installing Puppet, you can use it right away. Puppet is driven by manifests, the equivalent of scripts or programs, written in Puppet's **Domain-Specific Language** (**DSL**). Let's start with the obligatory `Hello, world!` manifest:

```
# hello_world.pp
notify { 'Hello, world!':
}
```

Downloading the example code:
You can download the example code files for all the Packt Publishing books you have purchased from your account at `http://www.packtpub.com`. If you purchased this book elsewhere, you can visit `http://www.packtpub.com/support` and register yourself to have the files emailed directly to you.

To put the manifest to work, use the following command (we avoided the term `execute` on purpose-manifests cannot be executed; more details will follow around the middle of this chapter):

```
root@puppetmaster:~# puppet apply hello_world.pp
Notice: Compiled catalog for puppetmaster.example.net in environment
production in 0.45 seconds
Notice: Hello, world!
Notice: /Stage[main]/Main/Notify[Hello, world!]/message: defined 'message'
as 'Hello, world!'
Notice: Applied catalog in 0.03 seconds
```

The package from Puppet Inc. bundles all required software components and installs to `/opt/puppetlabs`. In the case that the puppet command cannot be found, you can either specify the full path (`/opt/puppetlabs/bin/puppet`) or you can refresh your shell environment (`exec bash`, or log out and log in again).

Before we take a look at the structure of the manifest and the output from the `puppet apply` command, let's do something useful, just as an example. Puppet comes with its own background service. Let's assume that you want to learn the basics before letting it mess with your system. You can write a manifest to have Puppet make sure that the service is not currently running and will not be started at system boot:

```
# puppet_service.pp
service { 'puppet':
  ensure => 'stopped',
  enable => false,
}
```

To control system processes, boot options, software installation, and the same as the Puppet needs to be run with `root` privileges. This is the most common way to invoke the tool, because Puppet will often manage OS-level facilities. Apply your new manifest with root access, either through `sudo` or from a root shell, as shown in the following transcript:

```
root@puppetmaster:~# puppet apply puppet_service.pp
Notice: Compiled catalog for puppetmaster.example.net in environment
production in 0.61 seconds
Notice: /Stage[main]/Main/Service[puppet]/ensure: ensure changed 'running'
to 'stopped'
Notice: Applied catalog in 0.15 seconds
```

Now, Puppet has disabled the automatic startup of its background service for you. Applying the same manifest again has no effect, because the necessary steps are already complete:

```
root@puppetmaster:~# puppet apply puppet_service.pp
Notice: Compiled catalog for puppetmaster.example.net in environment
production in 0.62 seconds
Notice: Applied catalog in 0.07 seconds
```

This reflects a standard behavior in Puppet: Puppet resources are **idempotent**, which means that every resource first compares the actual (system) with the desired (Puppet) state and only initiates actions in case there is a difference (configuration drift).

You will often get this output from Puppet. It tells you that everything is as it should be. As such, this is a desirable outcome, like the all clean output from git status.

Introducing resources, parameters, and properties

Each of the manifests you wrote in the previous section declared one respective resource. Resources are the elementary building blocks of manifests. Each has a type (in this case, notify and service, respectively) and a name or title (Hello, world! and puppet). Each resource is unique to a manifest, and can be referenced by the combination of its type and name, such as Service["puppet"]. Finally, a resource also comprises a list of zero or more attributes. An attribute is a key-value pair, such as "enable => false".

Attribute names cannot be chosen arbitrarily. They are part of the Puppet resource type. Puppet differentiates between two different attributes: parameters and properties. Each resource type supports a specific set of attributes. Parameters describe the way that Puppet should deal with a resource type. Properties describe a specific setting of a resource. Certain parameters are available for all resource types (metaparameters), and some names are just very common, such as ensure. The service type supports the ensure property, which represents the status of the managed process. Its enabled property, on the other hand, relates to the system boot configuration (with respect to the service in question).

 We have used the terms attribute, property, and parameter in a seemingly interchangeable fashion. Don't be deceived-there are important distinctions. Property and parameter are the two different kinds of attributes that Puppet uses.

You have already seen two properties in action. Let's look at a parameter:

```
service { 'puppet':
  ensure   => 'stopped',
  enable   => false,
  provider => 'upstart',
}
```

The provider parameter tells Puppet that it needs to interact with the upstart subsystem to control its background service, as opposed to systemd or init. If you don't specify this parameter, Puppet makes an educated guess. There is quite a multitude of supported facilities to manage services on a system. You will learn more about providers and their automatic choosing later on.

The difference between parameters and properties is that the parameter merely indicates how Puppet should manage the resource, not what a desired state is. Puppet will only take action on property values. In this example, these are ensure => 'stopped' and enable => false. For each such property, Puppet will perform the following tasks:

- Test whether the resource is already in sync with the target state
- If the resource is not in sync, it will trigger a sync action

A property is considered to be in sync when the system entity that is managed by the given resource (in this case, the upstart service configuration for Puppet) is in the state that is described by the property value in the manifest. In this example, the ensure property will be in sync only if the puppet service is not running. The enable property is in sync if upstart is not configured to launch Puppet at system start.

As a mnemonic concerning parameters versus properties, just remember that properties can be out of sync, whereas parameters cannot.

Puppet also allows you to read your existing system state by using the puppet resource command:

```
root@puppetmaster:~# puppet resource user root
user { 'root':
  ensure              => 'present',
  comment             => 'root',
  gid                 => '0',
  home                => '/root',
  password            => '$6$17/7FtU/$TvYEDtFgGr0SaS7xOVloWXVTqQxxDUgH.
eBKJ7bgHJ.hdoc03Xrvm2ru0HFKpu1QSpVW/7o.rLdk/9MZANEGt/',
  password_max_age => '99999',
  password_min_age => '0',
  shell               => '/bin/bash',
  uid                 => '0',
}
```

Please note that some resource types will return read-only attributes (for example, the file resource type will return mtime and ctime). Refer to the appropriate type's documentation.

Interpreting output of the puppet apply command

As you have already witnessed, the output presented by Puppet is rather verbose. As you get more experienced with the tool, you will quickly learn to spot the crucial pieces of information. Let's first take a look at the informational messages, though. Apply the `service.pp` manifest once more:

```
root@puppetmaster:~# puppet apply puppet_service.pp
Notice: Compiled catalog for puppetmaster.example.net in environment
production in 0.48 seconds
Notice: Applied catalog in 0.05 seconds
```

Puppet took no particular action. You only get two timings: one from the compiling phase of the manifest, and the other from the catalog application phase. The catalog is a comprehensive representation of a compiled manifest. Puppet bases all its efforts concerning the evaluation and syncing of resources on the content of its current catalog.

Now, to quickly force Puppet to show you some more interesting output, pass it a one-line manifest directly from the shell. Regular users of Ruby or Perl will recognize the call syntax:

```
# puppet apply -e'service { "puppet": enable => true, }'
Notice: Compiled catalog for puppetmaster.example.net in environment
production in 0.62 seconds
Notice: /Stage[main]/Main/Service[puppet]/enable: enable changed 'false' to
'true'
Notice: Applied catalog in 0.12 seconds.
```

We prefer double quotes in manifests that get passed as command-line arguments, because on the shell, the manifest should be enclosed in single quotes as a whole.

You instructed Puppet to perform yet another change on the Puppet service. The output reflects the exact change that was performed. Let's analyze this log message:

- The `Notice:` keyword at the beginning of the line represents the log level. Other levels include `Warning`, `Error`, and `Debug`
- The property that changed is referenced with a whole path, starting with `Stage[main]`. Stages are beyond the scope of this book, so you will always just see the default of `main` here

- The next path element is `Main`, which is another default. It denotes the class in which the resource was declared. You will learn about classes in `Chapter 4`, *Combining Resources in Classes and Defined Types*
- Next, is the resource. You already learned that `Service[puppet]` is its unique reference
- Finally, `enable` is the name of the property in question. When several properties are out of sync, there will usually be one line of output for each property that gets synchronized
- The rest of the log line indicates the type of change that Puppet saw fit to apply. The wording depends on the nature of the property. It can be as simple as `created`, for a resource that is newly added to the managed system, or a short phrase, such as `changed false to true`

Dry testing your manifest

Another useful command-line switch for `puppet apply` is the `--noop` option.
It instructs Puppet to refrain from taking any action on unsynced resources.
Instead, you only get a log output that indicates what will change without the switch. This is useful in determining whether a manifest would possibly break anything on your system:

```
root@puppetmaster:~# puppet apply puppet_service.pp --noop
Notice: Compiled catalog for puppetmaster.example.net in environment
production in 0.63 seconds
Notice: /Stage[main]/Main/Service[puppet]/enable: current_value true,
should be false (noop)
Notice: Class[Main]: Would have triggered 'refresh' from 1 events
Notice: Stage[main]: Would have triggered 'refresh' from 1 events
Notice: Applied catalog in 0.06 seconds
```

The output format is the same as before, with a (noop) marker trailing the notice about the sync action. This log can be considered a preview of what will happen when the manifest is applied without the `--noop` switch.

The additional notices about triggered refreshes will be described later, and can be ignored for the moment. You will have a better understanding of their significance after finishing this chapter and `Chapter 4`, *Combining Resources in Classes and Defined Types*.

Using variables

Variable assignment works just like it does in most scripting languages. Any variable name is always prefixed with the $ sign:

```
$download_server = 'img2.example.net'
$url = "https://${download_server}/pkg/example_source.tar.gz"
```

Also, just like most scripting languages, Puppet performs variable value substitution in strings that are in double quotes, but no interpolation at all in single-quoted strings.

Variables are useful for making your manifest more concise and comprehensible. They help you with the overall goal of keeping your source code free from redundancy. An important distinction from variables in imperative programming and scripting languages is the immutability of variables in Puppet manifests. Once a value has been assigned, it cannot be overwritten.

Why is it called a variable at all if it is a constant? One should never look at Puppet as a tool that manages a single system. For a single system, a Puppet variable might look like a constant, but Puppet manages a multitude of systems with different operating systems. Across all these systems, variables will be different and not constants.

Variable types

As of Puppet 3.x, there are only four variable types: strings, arrays, hashes, and Booleans. Puppet 4 introduces a rich data type system. The new data type system will be explained at the end of, Chapter 7, *New Features from Puppet 4 and 5*. The basic variable types work much like their respective counterparts in other languages. Depending on your background, you might be familiar with using associative arrays or dictionaries as semantic equivalents to Puppet's hash type:

```
$a_bool = true
$a_string = 'This is a string value'
$an_array = [ 'This', 'forms', 'an', 'array' ]
$a_hash = {
  'subject'   => 'Hashes',
  'predicate' => 'are written',
  'object'    => 'like this',
  'note'      => 'not actual grammar!',
  'also note' => [ 'nesting is',
{ 'allowed'   => ' of course' } ],
}
```

Accessing the values is equally simple. Note that the hash syntax is similar to that of Ruby, not Perl:

```
$x = $a_string
$y = $an_array[1]
$z = $a_hash['object']
```

Strings can be used as resource attribute values, but it's worth noting that a resource title can also be a variable reference:

```
package { $apache_package:
  ensure => 'installed'
}
```

It's intuitively clear what a string value means in this context. But you can also pass arrays here to declare a whole set of resources in one statement. The following manifest manages three packages, making sure that they are all installed:

```
$packages = [
  'apache2',
  'libapache2-mod-php5',
  'libapache2-mod-passenger',
  ]
package { $packages:
  ensure => 'installed'
}
```

You will learn how to make efficient use of hash values in later chapters.

The array does not need to be stored in a variable to be used, but it is a good practice in some cases.

Data types

The data type system in Puppet 4 allows you to check and verify whether a variable is of a specific data type. This prevents code from behaving incorrectly when (for example) it expects an array but receives a Boolean value.

The full power of data types will be explained in Chapter 7, *New Features from Puppet 4 and 5*. Within Puppet manifests, it is possible to check for data types using the regexp control structure.

Puppet has core data types and abstract data types. The core data types are the most commonly used types of data, such as string or integer, whereas abstract data types allow for more sophisticated type validation, such as optional or variant.

Prior to dealing with data types, we must understand the concept of control structures within Puppet manifests.

Adding control structures in manifests

So far, you have written three simple manifests while following the instructions in this chapter. Each comprised only one resource, and one of them was given on the command line using the -e option. Of course, you would not want to write distinct manifests for each possible circumstance. Instead, just as how Ruby or Perl scripts branch out into different code paths, there are structures that make your Puppet code flexible and reusable for different circumstances.

The most common control element is the if/else block. It is quite similar to its equivalents in many programming languages:

```
if 'mail_lda' in $needed_services {
  service { 'dovecot': enable => true }
} else {
  service { 'dovecot': enable => false }
}
```

The Puppet DSL also has a case statement, which is reminiscent of its counterparts in other languages as well:

```
case $role {
  'imap_server': {
    package { 'dovecot': ensure => installed, }
    service { 'dovecot': ensure => running, }
  }
  /_webservers$/: {
    service { ['apache', 'ssh']: ensure => running, }
  }
  default: {
    service { 'ssh': ensure => running, }
  }
}
```

At the second matcher, you can see how it is possible to use regular expressions.

The case statement can also be used to switch to specific code based on variable data types:

```
case $role {
  Array: {
    include $role[0]
  }
  String: {
    include $role
  }
  default: {
    notify { 'This nodes $role variable is neither an
    Array nor a String':}
  }
}
```

A variation of the case statement is the selector. It's an expression, not a statement, and can be used in a fashion similar to the ternary if/else operator found in C-like languages:

```
package { 'dovecot':
  ensure => $role ? {
    'imap_server' => 'installed',
    /desktop$/    => 'purged',
    default       => 'removed',
  },
}
```

Similar to the case statement, the selector can also be used to return results, depending on the data types:

```
package { 'dovecot':
  ensure  => $role ? {
    Boolean => 'installed',
    String  => 'purged',
    default => 'removed',
  },
}
```

The selector should be used with caution, because in more complex manifests, this syntax will impede readability.

Controlling the order of execution

With what you've seen this far, you might have got the impression that Puppet's DSL is a specialized scripting language. That is actually quite far from the truth. A manifest is not a script or program. The language is a tool to model a system state through a set of resources, including files, packages, and cron jobs, among others.

The whole paradigm is different from that of scripting languages. Ruby or Perl are imperative languages that are based around statements that will be evaluated in a strict order. The Puppet DSL is declarative, which means that the manifest declares a set of resources that are expected to have certain properties. These resources are put into a catalog, and Puppet then tries to build a path through all declared resources. The compiler parses the manifests in order, but the configurer applies resources in a very different way.

In other words, the manifests should always describe what you expect to be the end result. The specifics of what actions need to be taken to get there are decided by Puppet.

To make this distinction more clear, let's look at an example:

```
package { 'haproxy':
  ensure => 'installed',
}
file {'/etc/haproxy/haproxy.cfg':
  ensure => file,
  owner  => 'root',
  group  => 'root',
  mode   => '0644',
  source => 'puppet:///modules/haproxy/etc/haproxy/haproxy.cfg',
}
service { 'haproxy':
  ensure => 'running',
}
```

With this manifest, Puppet will make sure that the following state is reached:

1. The `HAproxy` package is installed.
2. The `haproxy.cfg` file has specific content, which has been prepared in a file in `/etc/puppet/modules/`.
3. `HAproxy` is started.

To make this work, it is important that the necessary steps are performed in order:

- A configuration file cannot usually be installed before the package because there is not yet a directory to contain it
- The service cannot start before installation either. If it becomes active before the configuration is in place, it will use the default settings from the package instead

This point is being stressed because the preceding manifest does not, in fact, contain cues for Puppet to indicate such a strict ordering. Without explicit dependencies, Puppet is free to put the resources in any order it sees fit.

The recent versions of Puppet allow a form of local manifest-based ordering, so the presented example will actually work as is. The manifest-based ordering can be configured in the puppet.conf configuration file as follows:

```
ordering = manifest
```

This setting is default for Puppet 4. It is still important to be aware of the ordering principles because the implicit order is difficult to determine in more complex manifests, and as you will learn soon, there are other factors that will influence the order.

Declaring dependencies

The easiest way to bring order to such a straightforward manifest is resource chaining. The syntax for this is a simple ASCII arrow between two resources:

```
package { 'haproxy':
  ensure => 'installed',
}
->
file { '/etc/haproxy/haproxy.cfg':
  ensure => file,
  owner   => 'root',
  group   => 'root',
  mode    => '0644',
  source => 'puppet:///modules/haproxy/etc/haproxy/haproxy.cfg',
}
->
service {'haproxy':
  ensure => 'running',
}
```

This is only viable if all the related resources can be written next to each other. In other words, if the graphic representation of the dependencies does not form a straight chain, but more of a tree, star, or any other shape, this syntax is not sufficient.

> Internally, Puppet *will* construct an ordered graph of resources and synchronize them during a traversal of that graph.

A more generic and flexible way to declare dependencies is through special metaparameters-parameters that are eligible for use with any resource type. There are different metaparameters, most of which have nothing to do with ordering (you have seen `provider` in an earlier example). For resource ordering, Puppet offers the metaparameters require and before.

Both take one or more references to a declared resource as their value. As was previously mentioned, Puppet references have a special syntax:

```
Type['title']
e.g.
Package['haproxy']
```

> You can only build references to resources that are declared in the catalog. You cannot build and use references to something that is not managed by Puppet, even when it exists on the managed system.

Here is the `HAproxy` manifest, ordered using the `require` metaparameter:

```
package { 'haproxy':
  ensure   => 'installed',
}
file {'/etc/haproxy/haproxy.cfg':
  ensure   => file,
  owner    => 'root',
  group    => 'root',
  mode     => '0644',
  source   => 'puppet:///modules/haproxy/etc/haproxy/haproxy.cfg',
  require => Package['haproxy'],
}
  service {'haproxy':
  ensure   => 'running',
  require => File['/etc/haproxy/haproxy.cfg'],
}
```

The following manifest is semantically identical, but relies on the `before` metaparameter rather than `require`:

```
package { 'haproxy':
  ensure => 'installed',
  before => File['/etc/haproxy/haproxy.cfg'],
}
file { '/etc/haproxy/haproxy.cfg':
  ensure => file,
  owner  => 'root',
  group  => 'root',
  mode   => '0644',
  source => 'puppet:///modules/haproxy/etc/haproxy/haproxy.cfg',
  before => Service['haproxy'],
}
service { 'haproxy':
  ensure => 'running',
}
```

 The manifest can also mix both styles of notation, of course. This is left as a reader exercise with no dedicated depiction.

The `require` metaparameter usually leads to more understandable code because it expresses the dependency of the annotated resource on another resource. The `before` parameter, on the other hand, implies a dependency that a referenced resource forms upon the current resource. This can be counter-intuitive, especially for frequent users of packaging systems (which usually implement a `require`-style dependency declaration).

Sometimes, it might be difficult to decide whether to use `require` or `before`. In simple cases, most people prefer `require`. In some cases, it is easier to use `before`. Think of services that have multiple configuration files. Keeping information about the configuration file and the requirement in a single place reduces errors caused by forgetting to also adopt changes to the service when adding or removing additional configuration files. Take a look at the following example code:

```
file { '/etc/apache2/apache2.conf':
  ensure => file,
  before => Service['apache2'],
}
file { '/etc/apache2/httpd.conf':
  ensure => file,
  before => Service['apache2'],
}
service { 'apache2':
```

```
   ensure => running,
   enable => true,
}
```

In the example, all dependencies are declared within the file resource declarations. If you use the require parameter instead, you will always need to touch at least two resources in case of changes:

```
file { '/etc/apache2/apache2.conf':
  ensure => file,
}
file { '/etc/apache2/httpd.conf':
  ensure => file,
}
service { 'apache2':
  ensure => running,
  enable => true,
 require => [
    File['/etc/apache2/apache2.conf'],
    File['/etc/apache2/httpd.conf'],
  ],
}
```

Will you remember to update the service resource declaration whenever you add a new file to be managed by Puppet? Consider another, simpler example:

```
if $os_family == 'Debian' {
  file { '/etc/apt/preferences.d/example.net.prefs':
    content => '...',
    before  => Package['apache2'],
  }
}
package { 'apache2':
  ensure    => 'installed',
}
```

The file in the `preferences.d` directory only makes sense for Debian-like systems; that's why the package cannot safely `require` it. If the manifest is applied on a different OS, such as CentOS, the `apt` preferences file will not appear in the catalog thanks to the `if` clause. If the package had it as a requirement regardless, the resulting catalog would be inconsistent, and Puppet would not apply it. Specifying `before` in the file resource is safe, and semantically equivalent.

The `before` metaparameter is outright necessary in situations like this one, and can make the manifest code more elegant and straightforward in other scenarios. Familiarity with both `before` and `require` is advisable.

Error propagation

Defining requirements serves another important purpose. References on declared resources will only be validated as successful references if the depended-upon resource was finished successfully. This can be seen as a kind of stop point inside Puppet DSL code, when a required resource is not synchronized successfully.

For example, a `file` resource will fail if the URL of the `source` file is broken:

```
file { '/etc/haproxy/haproxy.cfg':
  ensure => file,
  source => 'puppet:///modules/haproxy/etc/haproxy.cfg',
}
```

One path segment is missing here. Puppet will report that the file resource could not be synchronized:

```
root@puppetmaster:~# puppet apply typo.pp
Notice: Compiled catalog for puppetmaster.example.net in environment
production in 0.62 seconds
Error: /Stage[main]/Main/File[/etc/haproxy/haproxy.cfg]: Could not
evaluate: Could not retrieve information from environment production
source(s) puppet:///modules/haproxy/etc/haproxy.cfg
Notice: /Stage[main]/Main/Service[haproxy]: Dependency
File[/etc/haproxy/haproxy.cfg] has failures: true
Warning: /Stage[main]/Main/Service[haproxy]: Skipping because of failed
dependencies
Notice: Applied catalog in 0.06 seconds
```

In this example, the `Error` line describes the error caused by the broken URL. The error propagation is represented by the `Notice` and `Warning` lines below it.

Puppet failed to apply changes to the configuration file; it cannot compare the current state to the nonexistent source. As the service depends on the configuration file, Puppet will not even try to start it. This is for safety: if any dependencies cannot be put into the defined state, Puppet must assume that the system is not fit for the application of the dependent resource.

This is another important reason to make use of resource dependencies. Remember that both the chaining arrow and the `before` metaparameter imply error propagation as well.

Avoiding circular dependencies

Before you learn about another way in which resources can interrelate, there is an issue that you should be aware of: dependencies must not form circles. Let's visualize this in an example:

```
file { '/etc/haproxy':
  ensure  => 'directory',
  owner   => 'root',
  group   => 'root',
  mode    => '0644',
}
file { '/etc/haproxy/haproxy.cfg':
  ensure  => file,
  owner   => 'root',
  group   => 'root',
  mode    => '0644',
  source  => 'puppet:///modules/haproxy/etc/haproxy/haproxy.cfg',
}
service { 'haproxy':
  ensure  => 'running',
  require => File['/etc/haproxy/haproxy.cfg'],
  before  => File['/etc/haproxy'],
}
```

The dependency circle in this manifest is somewhat hidden (as will likely be the case for many such circles that you will encounter during regular use of Puppet).
It is formed by the following relations:

- The `File['/etc/haproxy/haproxy.cfg']` auto-requires the parent directory, `File['/etc/haproxy']`. This is an implicit, built-in dependency
- The parent directory, `File['/etc/haproxy']`, requires `Service['haproxy']` due to its `before` metaparameter
- The `Service['haproxy']` service requires the `File['/etc/haproxy/haproxy.cfg']` config

Implicit dependencies exist for the following resource combinations, among others:

- If a directory and a file inside the `directory` are declared, Puppet will first create the `directory` and then the file
- If a user and his/her primary group is declared, Puppet will first create the group and then the user
- If a file and the owner (user) are declared, Puppet will first create the user and then the file

Granted, the preceding example is contrived-it will not make sense to manage the service before the configuration directory. Nevertheless, even a manifest design that is apparently sound can result in circular dependencies. This is how Puppet will react to such a design:

```
root@puppetmaster:~# puppet apply circle.pp
Notice: Compiled catalog for puppetmaster.example.net in environment
production in 0.62 seconds
Error: Failed to apply catalog: Found 1 dependency cycle:
(File[/etc/haproxy/haproxy.cfg] =>
            Service[haproxy] =>
        File[/etc/haproxy] => File[/etc/haproxy/haproxy.cfg])
Try the '--graph' option and opening the resulting '.dot' file in
OmniGraffle or GraphViz
```

The output helps you locate the offending relation(s). For very wide dependency circles with lots of involved resources, the textual rendering is difficult to analyze. Therefore, Puppet also gives you the opportunity to get a graphical representation of the dependency graph through the `--graph` option.

If you do this, Puppet will include the full path to the newly created `.dot` file in its output. Its content looks similar to Puppet's output:

```
digraph Resource_Cycles {
label = "Resource Cycles"
"File[/etc/haproxy/haproxy.cfg]" ->"Service[haproxy]"
->"File[/etc/haproxy]" ->"File[/etc/haproxy/haproxy.cfg]"
}
```

This is not helpful by itself, but it can be fed directly into tools such as `dotty` to produce an actual diagram.

To summarize, resource dependencies are helpful in keeping Puppet from acting upon resources in unexpected or uncontrolled situations. They are also useful in restricting the order of resource evaluation.

Implementing resource interaction

In addition to dependencies, resources can also enter a similar yet different mutual relation. Remember the pieces of output that we skipped earlier. They are as follows:

```
root@puppetmaster:~# puppet apply puppet_service.pp --noop
Notice: Compiled catalog for puppetmaster.example.net in environment
production in 0.62 seconds
Notice: /Stage[main]/Main/Service[puppet]/ensure: current_value running,
should be stopped (noop)
Notice: Class[Main]: Would have triggered 'refresh' from 1 events
Notice: Stage[main]: Would have triggered 'refresh' from 1 events
Notice: Applied catalog in 0.05 seconds
```

Puppet mentions that **refreshes** would have been triggered for the reason of an **event**. Such events are emitted by resources whenever Puppet acts on the need for a sync action. Without explicit code to receive and react to events, they just get discarded.

The mechanism to set up such event receivers is named in an analogy of a generic publish/subscribe queue; resources get configured to react to events using the `subscribe` metaparameter. There is no `publish` keyword or parameter, since each and every resource is technically a publisher of events (messages). Instead, the counterpart of the `subscribe` metaparameter is called `notify`, and it explicitly directs generated events at referenced resources.

One of the most common practical uses of the event system is to reload service configurations. When a `service` resource consumes an event (usually from a change in a config file), Puppet invokes the appropriate action to make the service restart.

If you instruct Puppet to do this, it can result in brief service interruptions due to this restart operation. Note that if the new configuration causes an error, the service might fail to start and stay offline.

The following code example shows the relationships between the `haproxy` package, the corresponding `haproxy` configuration file, and the `haproxy` service:

```
file { '/etc/haproxy/haproxy.cfg':
  ensure  => file,
  owner   => 'root',
  group   => 'root'
  mode    => '0644'
  source  => 'puppet:///modules/haproxy/etc/haproxy/haproxy.cfg',
  require => Package['haproxy'],
}
```

```
service { 'haproxy':
  ensure    => 'running',
  subscribe => File['/etc/haproxy/haproxy.cfg'],
}
```

If the `notify` metaparameter is to be used instead, it must be specified for the resource that emits the event:

```
file { '/etc/haproxy/haproxy.cfg':
  ensure  => file,
  owner   => 'root',
  group   => 'root',
  mode    => '0644',
  source  => 'puppet:///modules/haproxy/etc/haproxy/haproxy.cfg',
  require => Package['haproxy'],
  notify  => Service['haproxy'],
}
service { 'haproxy':
  ensure  => 'running',
}
```

This will likely feel reminiscent of the `before` and `require` metaparameters, which offer symmetrical ways of expressing an interrelation of a pair of resources just as well. This is not a coincidence, these metaparameters are closely related to each other:

- The resource that subscribes to another resource implicitly requires it
- The resource that notifies another is implicitly placed before the later one in the dependency graph

In other words, `subscribe` is the same as `require`, except for the dependent resource receiving events from its peer. The same holds true for `notify` and `before`.

The chaining syntax is also available for signaling. To establish a signaling relation between neighboring resources, use an ASCII arrow with a tilde, `~>`, instead of the dash in `->`:

```
file { '/etc/haproxy/haproxy.cfg': ... }
~>
service { 'haproxy': ... }
```

The `service` resource type is one of the two notable types that support refreshing when resources get notified (the other will be discussed in the next section). There are others, but they are not as ubiquitous.

Examining Puppet core resource types

To complete our tour of the basic elements of a manifest, let's take a closer look at the resource types that you have already used, and some of the more important ones that you have not yet encountered and are part of Puppet's base installation.

You probably already have a good feeling for the `file` type, which will ensure the existence of files and directories, along with their permissions. Pulling a file from a repository (usually, a Puppet module) using the `source` parameter is also a frequent use case.

For very short files, it is more economical to include the desired content right in the manifest:

```
file { '/etc/modules':
  ensure  => file,
  content => "# Managed by Puppet!\n\ndrbd\n",
}
```

The double quotes allow expansion of escape sequences, such as \n.

Another useful capability is managing symbolic links:

```
file { '/etc/apache2/sites-enabled/001-puppet-lore.org':
  ensure => 'link',
  target => '../sites-available/puppet-lore.org',
}
```

You should be aware that the file resource type requires an absolute path and filename. If a relative path is used within the title, then Puppet will produce an error:

```
file { '../demo.txt':
  ensure => file,
}
```

```
puppet apply file_error.pp
Notice: Compiled catalog for puppetmaster.demo.example42.com in environment
production in 0.09 seconds
Error: Parameter path failed on File[../demo.txt]: File paths must be fully
qualified, not '../demo.txt' at /root/file_error.pp:1
```

The next type that you already know is `package`, and its typical usage is quite intuitive. Make sure that packages are either installed or removed. A notable use case that you have not yet seen is to use the basic package manager instead of `apt` or `yum`/`zypper`. This is useful if the package is not available from a repository:

```
package { 'haproxy':
  ensure   => present,
  provider => 'dpkg',
  source   => '/opt/packages/haproxy-1.5.1_amd64.dpkg',
}
```

Your mileage usually increases if you make the effort of setting up a simple repository instead, so that the main package manager can be used after all.

Last but not least, there is a `service` type, the most important attributes of which you already know. It's worth pointing out that it can serve as a simple shortcut in cases where you don't wish to add a fully-fledged `init` script or something similar. With enough information, the `base` provider for the `service` type will manage simple background processes for you:

```
service { 'count-logins':
  provider     => 'base',
  ensure       => 'running',
  enable       => true,
  binary       => '/usr/local/bin/cnt-logins',
  start        => '/usr/local/bin/cnt-logins -daemonize',
  has_status   => true,
  has_restart  => true,
  subscribe    => File['/usr/local/bin/cnt-logins'],
}
```

Puppet will not only restart the script if it is not running for some reason, but will also restart it whenever the content of the referenced configuration file changes.
This only works if Puppet manages the file content and all changes propagate through Puppet only.

 If Puppet changes any other property of the script file (for example, the file mode), that too will lead to a restart of the process.

Let's take a look at some other types you will probably need.

The user and group types

Especially in the absence of central registries, such as LDAP, it is useful to be able to manage user accounts on each of your machines. There are providers for all supported platforms; however, the available attributes vary. On Linux, the useradd provider is the most common. It allows the management of all fields in /etc/passwd, such as uid and shell, and also group memberships:

```
group { 'proxy-admins':
  ensure      => present,
  gid         => 4002,
}
user { 'john':
  ensure      => present,
  uid         => 2014,
  home        => '/home/john',
  managehome  => true, # <- adds -m to useradd
  gid         => 1000,
  shell       => '/bin/zsh',
  groups      => [ 'proxy-admins' ],
}
```

As with all resources, Puppet will not only make sure that the user and group exist, but also fix any divergent properties, such as the home directory.

Even though the user depends on the group: (because it cannot be added before the group exists), it need not be expressed in the manifest. The user automatically requires all necessary groups, similar to a file auto-requiring its parent directory.

 Puppet will also happily manage your LDAP user accounts.

It was mentioned earlier that there are different attributes available, depending on the operating system. Linux (and the useradd provider) support setting a password, whereas on HP-UX (using the hp-ux provider), the user password cannot be set via Puppet.

In this case, Puppet will only show a warning saying that the user resource type is making use of an unsupported attribute, and will continue managing all other attributes. In other words, using an unsupported attribute in your Puppet DSL code will not break your Puppet run.

The exec resource type

There is one oddball resource type in the Puppet core. Remember our earlier assertion that Puppet is not a specialized scripting engine, but a tool that allows you to model part of your system state in a compelling DSL, and which is capable of altering your system to meet the defined goal. This is why you declare user and group, instead of invoking groupadd and useradd in order. You can do this because Puppet comes with support to manage such entities. This is vastly beneficial because Puppet also knows that, on different platforms, other commands are used for account management, and that the arguments can be subtly different on some systems.

Of course, Puppet does not have knowledge of all the conceivable particulars of any supported system. Say that you wish to manage an OpenAFS file server. There are no specific resource types to aid you with this. The ideal solution is to exploit Puppet's plugin system and to write your own types and providers so that your manifests can just reflect the AFS-specific configuration. This is not simple, though, and also not worthwhile in cases where you only need Puppet to invoke some exotic commands from very few places in your manifest.

For such cases, Puppet ships with the exec resource type, which allows the execution of custom commands in lieu of an abstract sync action.

For example, it can be used to unpack a tar ball in the absence of a proper package:

```
exec { 'tar cjf /opt/packages/homebrewn-3.2.tar.bz2':
  cwd     => '/opt',
  path    => '/bin:/usr/bin',
  creates => '/opt/homebrewn-3.2',
}
```

The `creates` parameter is important for Puppet to tell whether the command needs running. Once the specified path exists, the resource counts as synchronized. For commands that do not create a telltale file or directory, there are the alternative parameters, `onlyif` and `unless`, to allow Puppet to query the sync state:

```
exec { 'perl -MCPAN -e "install YAML"':
  path   => '/bin:/usr/bin',
  unless => 'cpan -l | grep -qP ^YAML\\b',
}
```

The query command's exit code determines the state. In the case of `unless`, the `exec` command runs if the query fails. This is how the `exec` type maintains idempotency. Puppet does this automatically for most resource types, but this is not possible for `exec` because synchronization is defined so arbitrarily. It becomes your responsibility as the user to define the appropriate queries per resource.

Finally, the `exec` type resources are the second notable case of receivers for events using `notify` and `subscribe`:

```
exec { 'apt-get update':
  path        => '/bin:/usr/bin',
  subscribe   => File['/etc/apt/sources.list.d/jenkins.list'],
  refreshonly => true,
}
```

You can even chain multiple `exec` resources in this fashion so that each invocation triggers the next one. However, this is bad practice, and degrades Puppet to a (rather flawed) scripting engine. The `exec` resources should be avoided in favor of regular resources whenever possible. Some resource types that are not part of the core are available as plugins from the Puppet Forge. You will learn more about this topic in `Chapter 5`, *Combining Classes, Configuration Files, and Extensions into Modules*.

Since `exec` resources can be used to perform virtually *any* operation, they are sometimes abused to stand in for more proper resource types. This is a typical antipattern in Puppet manifests. It is safer to regard `exec` resources as the last resort or emergency exit that is only to be used if all other alternatives have been exhausted.

Ideally, your `exec` resource types are built as one-time only commands.

All Puppet installations have the type documentation built into the code, which is printable on the command line by using the puppet describe command:

`puppet describe <type> [-s]`

In case you are unsure whether a type exists, you can tell puppet describe to return a full list of all available resource types:

puppet describe --list

Let's briefly discuss two more types that are supported out of the box. They allow the management of cron jobs, mounted partitions, and shares respectively, which are all frequent requirements in server operations.

The cron resource type

A cron job mainly consists of a command and the recurring time and date at which to run the command. Puppet models the command and each date particle as a property of a resource with the `cron` type:

```
cron { 'clean-files':
  ensure      => present,
  user        => 'root',
  command     => '/usr/local/bin/clean-files',
  minute      => '1',
  hour        => '3',
  weekday     => [ '2', '6' ],
  environment => 'MAILTO=felix@example.net',
}
```

The `environment` property allows you to specify one or more variable bindings for `cron` to add to the job.

The mount resource type

Finally, Puppet will manage all aspects of mountable filesystems for you, including their basic attributes, such as the source device and mount point, the mount options, and the current state. A line from the `fstab` file translates quite literally to a Puppet manifest:

```
mount { '/media/gluster-data':
  ensure => 'mounted',
  device => 'gluster01:/data',
```

```
    fstype  => 'glusterfs',
    options => 'defaults,_netdev',
    dump    => 0,
    pass    => 0,
}
```

For this resource, Puppet will make sure that the filesystem is indeed mounted after the run. Ensuring the unmounted state is also possible, of course; Puppet can also just make sure the entry is present in the fstab file, or absent from the system altogether.

Summary

After installing Puppet on your system, you can use it by writing and applying manifests. These manifests are written in Puppet's DSL and contain descriptions of the desired state of your system. Even though they resemble scripts, they should not be considered as such. For one thing, they consist of resources instead of commands. These resources are generally not evaluated in the order in which they have been written. An explicit ordering should be defined through the require and before metaparameters instead.

Each resource has a couple of attributes: parameters and properties. Each property is evaluated in its own right; Puppet detects whether a change to the system is necessary to get any property into the state that is defined in the manifest. It will also perform such changes. This is referred to as synchronizing a resource or property.

The ordering parameters, require and before, are of further importance because they establish dependency of one resource on one or more others. This allows Puppet to skip parts of the catalog if an important resource cannot be synchronized. Circular dependencies must be avoided.

Each resource in the manifest has a resource type that describes the nature of the system entity that is being managed. Some of the types that are used most frequently are file, package, and service. Puppet comes with many types for convenient system management, and many plugins are available to add even more. Some tasks require the use of exec resources, but this should be done sparingly.

In Chapter 2, *Puppet Server and Agents*, we will introduce the master/agent setup.

2
Puppet Server and Agents

So far, you have dealt with some concise Puppet manifests that were built to model some very specific goals. By means of the `puppet apply` command, you can use such snippets on any machine in your infrastructure. This is not the most common way of using Puppet, though, and this chapter will introduce you to the popular server/agent structure. It's worth noting, however, that applying standalone manifests that are independent of your overall Puppet design can always be useful.

Under the server/agent paradigm, you will typically install the Puppet agent software on all nodes under your care and make them call the server, which is yet another Puppet installation. The server will compile the appropriate manifests and effectively remotely control the agents. Both the agent and the server authenticate themselves using trusted SSL certificates.

This chapter covers the following topics:

- The Puppet server
- Setting up the Puppet agent
- Performance optimizations
- Completing the stack with PuppetDB
- The Puppet CA

The Puppet server

Many Puppet-based workflows are centered on the server, which is the central source of configuration data and authority. The server hands instructions to all the computer systems in the infrastructure (where agents are installed). It serves multiple purposes in the distributed system of Puppet components.

The server will perform the following tasks:

- Storing manifests and compiling catalogs
- Serving as the SSL certification authority
- Processing reports from the agent machines
- Gathering and storing information about the agents

As such, the security of your server machine is paramount. The requirements for hardening are comparable to those of a Kerberos key distribution center.

During its first initialization, the Puppet server generates the CA certificate. This self-signed certificate will be distributed among and trusted by all the components of your infrastructure. This is why its private key must be protected very carefully. New agent machines request individual certificates, which are signed with the CA certificate.

 It's a good idea to include a copy of the CA certificate in your OS-provisioning process so that the agent can establish the authenticity of the master before requesting its individual certificate.

The terminology around the master software might be a little confusing. That's because both the terms **Puppet master** and **Puppet server** are floating around, and they are closely related too. Let's consider some technological background in order to give you a better understanding of what is what.

Puppet's master service mainly comprises a RESTful HTTP API. Agents initiate the HTTPS transactions, with both sides identifying each other using trusted SSL certificates. During the time when Puppet 3 and older versions were the most advanced versions available, the HTTPS layer was typically handled by Apache. Puppet's Ruby core was invoked through the `Passenger` module. This approach offered good stability and scalability.

Puppet Inc. has improved upon this standard solution with specialized software called `puppetserver`. The Ruby-based core of the master remains basically unchanged, although it now runs on JRuby instead of Ruby's own MRI. The HTTPS layer is run by Jetty, sharing the same Java virtual machine with the master.

By cutting out some middlemen, `puppetserver` is faster and more scalable than a Passenger solution. It is also significantly easier to set up.

Setting up the server machine

Getting the `puppetserver` software onto a Linux machine is just as simple as the agent package (which you did at the very beginning of `Chapter 1`, *Writing Your First Manifests*). Packages are available on Red Hat Enterprise Linux and its derivatives, Debian and Ubuntu, and any other operating system that is supported to run a Puppet server.

Until now, the Puppet server must run on a Linux-based operating system, and cannot run on Windows or any other Unix. A great way to get Puppet Inc. packages on any platform is the Puppet Collection. Shortly after the release of Puppet 4, Puppet Inc. created this new way of supplying software. This can be considered as a distribution in its own right. Unlike Linux distributions, it does not contain a Kernel, system tools, or libraries. Instead, it comprises various software from the Puppet ecosystem. Software versions that are available from the same Puppet collection are guaranteed to work well together.

Use the following commands to install `puppetserver` from the first **Puppet Collection** (**PC1**) on a Debian 8 machine (the collection for Debian 9 has not yet received a `puppetserver` package at the time of writing this):

```
root@puppetmaster# wget
http://apt.puppetlabs.com/puppetlabs-release-pc1-jessie.deb
root@puppetmaster# dpkg -i puppetlabs-release-pc1-jessie.deb
root@puppetmaster# apt-get update
root@puppetmaster# apt-get install puppetserver
```

The `puppetserver` package comprises only the Jetty server and the Clojure API, but the all-in-one `puppet-agent` package is pulled in as a dependency.

> The package name, `puppet-agent`, is misleading. This AIO package contains all the parts of Puppet, including the master core, a vendored Ruby build, and several pieces of additional software.

Specifically, you can use the `puppet` command on the master node. You will soon learn how this is useful. However, when using the packages from Puppet Labs, everything gets installed under `/opt/puppetlabs`. It is advisable to make sure that your `PATH` variable always includes the `/opt/puppetlabs/bin` directory so that the `puppet` command is found here.

Regardless of this, once the `puppetserver` package is installed, you can start the master service:

```
root@puppetmaster# systemctl start puppetserver
```

Depending on the power of your machine, the startup can take a few minutes. Once initialization completes, the server will operate very smoothly, though. As soon as the master port `8140` is open, your Puppet master is ready to serve requests.

If the service fails to start, there might be an issue with certificate generation (we observed such issues with some versions of the software). Check the log file at `/var/log/puppetlabs/puppetserver/puppetserver-daemon.log`. If it indicates that there are problems while looking up its certificate file, you can work around the problem by temporarily running a standalone master as follows:

```
puppet master --no-daemonize
```

After initialization, you can stop this process. The certificate is available now, and `puppetserver` should now be able to start as well.

Another reason for start failures is an insufficient amount of memory. The Puppet server process needs 2 GB of memory.

Creating the master manifest

When you used Puppet locally in Chapter 1, *Writing Your First Manifests*, you specified a manifest file that `puppet apply` should compile. The master compiles manifests for many machines, but the agent does not get to choose which source file is to be used; this is completely at the master's discretion. The starting point for any compilation by the master is always the site manifest, which can be found in `/opt/puppetlabs/code/environments/production/manifests/`.

The significance of the environments/production part will be investigated in `Chapter 5`, *Combining Classes, Configuration Files, and Extensions into Modules*. In Puppet versions before 4.0, the site manifest is at another location, `/etc/puppet/manifests/site.pp`, and comprises just one file.

Each connecting agent will use all the manifests found here. Of course, you don't want to manage only one identical set of resources on all your machines. To define a piece of manifest exclusively for a specific agent, put it in a `node` block. This block's contents will only be considered when the calling agent has a matching common name in its SSL certificate. You can dedicate a piece of the manifest to a machine with the name of `agent`, for example:

```
node 'agent' {
  $packages = [ 'apache2',
    'libapache2-mod-php5',
    'libapache2-mod-passenger', ]
  package { $packages:
    ensure => 'installed',
    before => Service['apache2'],
  }
  service { 'apache2':
    ensure => 'running',
    enable => true,
  }
}
```

The given example does not show best practice for node classification. It is merely used as an example. We will show the modern best practice node classification in `Chapter 9`, *Puppet Roles and Profiles*.

Before you set up and connect your first agent to the master, step back and think about how the master should be addressed. By default, agents will try to resolve the unqualified `puppet` hostname in order to get the master's address. If you have a default domain that is being searched by your machines, you can use this as a default and add a record for `puppet` as a subdomain (such as `puppet.example.net`).

Otherwise, pick a domain name that seems fitting to you, such as `master.example.net` or `adm01.example.net`. What's important is the following:

- All your agent machines can resolve the name to an address
- The master process is listening for connections on that address
- The master uses a certificate with the chosen name as CN or DNS Alt Names

The mode of resolution depends on your circumstances; the `hosts` file on each machine is one ubiquitous possibility. The Puppet server listens on all the available addresses by default.

This leaves the task of creating a suitable certificate, which is simple. Configure the master to use the appropriate certificate name and restart the service. If the certificate does not exist yet, Puppet will take the necessary steps to create it. Put the following setting into your `/etc/puppetlabs/puppet/puppet.conf` file on the master machine:

```
[main]
certname=puppetmaster.example.net
```

In Puppet versions earlier than 4.0, the default location for the configuration file is `/etc/puppet/puppet.conf`.

Upon its next start, the master will use the appropriate certificate for all SSL connections. The automatic proliferation of SSL data is not dangerous, even in an existing setup, except for the certification authority. If the master were to generate a new CA certificate at any point in time, it would break the trust of all existing agents.

Make sure that the CA data is neither lost nor compromised. All previously signed certificates become obsolete whenever Puppet needs to create a new certification authority. The default storage location is `/etc/puppetlabs/puppet/ssl/ca` for Puppet 4.0 and higher, and `/var/lib/puppet/ssl/ca` for older versions.

Inspecting the configuration settings

All the customization of the master's parameters can be made in the `puppet.conf` file. The operating system packages ship with some settings that are deemed sensible by the respective maintainers. Apart from these explicit settings, Puppet relies on defaults that are either built-in or derived from the environment (details on how this works follow in the `Chapter 3`, *A Peek into the Ruby Part of Puppet - Facts, Types, and Providers*):

```
root@puppetmaster # puppet master --configprint manifest
/etc/puppetlabs/code/environments/production/manifests
```

Most users will want to rely on these defaults for as many settings as possible. This is possible without any drawbacks because Puppet makes all settings fully transparent using the `--configprint` parameter. For example, you can find out where the master manifest files are located.

To get an overview of all available settings and their values, use the following command:

```
root@puppetmaster# puppet master --configprint all | less
```

While this command is especially useful on the master side, the same introspection is available for `puppet apply` and `puppet agent`.

Setting specific configuration entries is possible with the `puppet config` command:

```
root@puppetmaster # puppet config set --section main certname
puppetmaster.example.net
```

Setting up the Puppet agent

As was explained earlier, the master mainly serves instructions to agents in the form of catalogs that are compiled from the manifest. You have also prepared a `node` block for your first agent in the master manifest.

Installing the agent software is easy; you did this at the start of `Chapter 1`, *Writing Your First Manifests*. The plain Puppet package that allows you to apply a local manifest contains all the required parts in order to operate a proper agent.

If you are using Puppet Labs packages, use the instructions from earlier in this chapter. On agent machines, you need not install the `puppetserver` package. Just get `puppet-agent` instead.

After a successful package installation, one needs to specify where puppet agent can find the puppet server:

```
root@puppetmaster # puppet config set --section agent server pup-
petmaster.example.net
```

Afterwards, the following invocation is sufficient for an initial test:

```
root@agent# puppet agent --test
Info: Creating a new SSL key for agent
Error: Could not request certificate: getaddrinfo: Name or service not
known
Exiting; failed to retrieve certificate and waitforcert is disabled
```

Puppet first created a new SSL certificate key for itself. For its own name, it picked `agent`, which is the machine's hostname. That's fine for now. An error occurred because the `puppet` name cannot be currently resolved to anything. Add this to `/etc/hosts` so that Puppet can contact the master:

```
root@agent# puppet agent --test
Info: Caching certificate for ca
Info: csr_attributes file loading from
/etc/puppetlabs/puppet/csr_attributes.yaml
Info: Creating a new SSL certificate request for agent
Info: Certificate Request fingerprint (SHA256):
52:65:AE:24:5E:2A:C6:17:E2:5D:0A:C9:
86:E3:52:44:A2:EC:55:AE:3D:40:A9:F6:E1:28:31:50:FC:8E:80:69
Exiting; failed to retrieve certificate and waitforcert is disabled
```

 How Puppet conveniently downloaded and cached the CA certificate. The agent will establish trust based on this certificate from now on.

Puppet created a certificate request and sent it to the master. It then immediately tried to download the signed certificate. This is expected to fail the master won't just sign a certificate for any request it receives. This behavior is important for proper security. There is a configuration setting that enables such automatic signing, but users are generally discouraged from using this setting because it allows the creation of arbitrary numbers of signed (and therefore, trusted) certificates to any user who has network access to the master.

To authorize the agent, look for the CSR on the master using the `puppet cert` command:

```
root@puppetmaster# puppet cert --list
"agent" (SHA256)
52:65:AE:24:5E:2A:C6:17:E2:5D:0A:C9:86:E3:52:44:A2:EC:55:AE:
3D:40:A9:F6:E1:28:31:50:FC:8E:80:69
```

This looks alright, so now you can sign a new certificate for the agent:

```
root@puppetmaster# puppet cert --sign agent
Notice: Signed certificate request for agent
Notice: Removing file Puppet::SSL::CertificateRequest agent at
'/etc/puppetlabs/ puppet/ssl/ca/requests/agent.pem'
```

When choosing the action for `puppet cert`, the dashes in front of the option name can be omitted; you can just use `puppet cert list` and `puppet cert sign`.

Now the agent can receive its certificate for its catalog run as follows:

```
root@agent# puppet agent --test
Info: Caching certificate for agent
Info: Caching certificate_revocation_list for ca
Info: Caching certificate for agent
Info: Retrieving pluginfacts
Info: Retrieving plugin
Info: Caching catalog for agent
Info: Applying configuration version '1437065761'
Notice: Applied catalog in 0.11 seconds
```

The agent is now fully operational. It received a catalog and applied all resources found within. Before you read on to learn how the agent usually operates, there is a note that is especially important for the users of Puppet 3.

Remember that you configured the master to use the name `master.example.net` for the master machine earlier in this chapter by setting the `certname` option in the master's `puppet.conf` file.

Since this is the common name in the master's certificate, the preceding command will not even work with a Puppet 3.x master. It works with `puppetserver` and Puppet 4 because the default `puppet` name is now included in the certificate's Subject Alternative Names by default.

It is tidier to not rely on this alias name, though. After all, in production, you will probably want to make sure that the master has a fully qualified name that can be resolved, at least inside your network. You should, therefore, add the following to the `main` section of `puppet.conf` on each agent machine:

```
[agent]
server=master.example.net
```

In the absence of DNS to resolve this name, your agent will need an appropriate entry in its hosts file or a similar alternative way of address resolution.

These steps are necessary in a Puppet 3.x setup. If you have been following along with a Puppet 4 agent, you might notice that after this change, it generates a new certificate signing request:

```
root@agent# puppet agent –test
Info:.Creating a new SSL key for agent.example.net
Info: csr_attributes file loading from
/etc/puppetlabs/puppet/csr_attributes.yaml
Info: Creating a new SSL certificate request for agent.example.net
Info: Certificate Request fingerprint (SHA256):
85:AC:3E:D7:6E:16:62:BD:28:15:B6:18:
12:8E:5D:1C:4E:DE:DF:C3:4E:8F:3E:20:78:1B:79:47:AE:36:98:FD
Exiting; no certificate found and waitforcert is disabled
```

If this happens, you will have to use `puppet cert sign` on the master again. The agent will then retrieve a new certificate.

The agent's life cycle

In a Puppet-centric workflow, you typically want all changes to the configuration of servers (perhaps even workstations) to originate on the Puppet master and propagate to the agents automatically. Each new machine gets integrated into the Puppet infrastructure with the master at its center, and gets removed during the decommissioning, as shown in the following diagram:

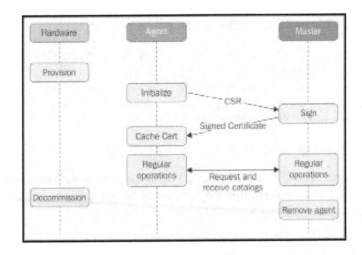

The very first step, generating a key and a certificate signing request is always performed implicitly and automatically at the start of an agent run if no local SSL data exists yet. Puppet creates the required data if no appropriate files are found. There will be a short description on how to trigger this behavior manually later in this section.

The next step is usually the signing of the agent's certificate, which is performed on the master. It is good practice to monitor the pending requests by listing them on the console:

```
root@puppetmaster# puppet cert list
root@puppetmaster# puppet cert sign '<agent fqdn>'
```

From this point on, the agent will periodically check with the master to load updated catalogs. The default interval for this is 30 minutes. The agent will perform a run of a catalog each time and check the sync state of all the contained resources. The run is performed for unchanged catalogs as well, because the sync states can change between runs.

 Before you manage to sign the certificate, the agent process will query the master at short intervals for a while. This can avoid a 30 minute delay if the certificate is not ready right when the agent starts up.

Launching this background process can be done manually through a simple command:

```
root@agent# puppet agent
```

However, it is preferable to do this through the `puppet` system service.

When an agent machine is taken out of active service, its certificate should be invalidated. As is customary with SSL, this is done through revocation and cleaning the certificate. The master adds the serial number of the certificate to its certificate revocation list. This list, too, is shared with each agent machine. Revocation is initiated on the master through the `puppet cert` command:

```
root@puppetmaster# puppet cert revoke agent
```

 The updated CRL is not honored until the master service is restarted. If security is a concern, this step must not be postponed.

The agent can then no longer use its old certificate:

```
root@agent# puppet agent --test
Warning: Unable to fetch my node definition, but the agent run will
continue:
Warning: SSL_connect SYSCALL returned=5 errno=0 state=unknown state
[...]
Error: Could not retrieve catalog from remote server: SSL_connect SYSCALL
returned=5 errno=0 state=unknown state
[...]
```

Renewing an agent's certificate

Sometimes, it is necessary during an agent machine's life cycle to regenerate its certificate and related data. The reasons for this can include data loss, human error, or certificate expiration, among others. The regeneration is achieved through the following steps:

1. Performing the regeneration is quite simple: all relevant files are kept at `/etc/puppetlabs/puppet/ssl` (for Puppet 3.x, this is `/var/lib/puppet/ssl`) on the agent machine.

2. Once these files are removed (or rather, the whole `ssl/` directory tree), Puppet will renew everything on the next agent run. Of course, a new certificate must be signed. This requires some preparation; just initiating the request from the agent will fail:

```
root@agent# puppet agent -test
Info: Creating a new SSL key for agent
Info: Caching certificate for ca
Info: Caching certificate for agent.example.net
```

```
Error: Could not request certificate: The certificate
retrievedfrom the master does not match the agent's private
key.
Certificate fingerprint:
6A:9F:12:C8:75:C0:B6:10:45:ED:C3:97:24:CC:98:F2:B6:1A:B5:
4C:E3:98:96:4F:DA:CD:5B:59:E0:7F:F5:E6
```

The master still has the old certificate cached. This is a simple protection against the impersonation of your agents by unauthorized entities.

3. To fix this, remove the certificate from both the master and the agent and then start a Puppet run, which will automatically regenerate a certificate:
   - On the master, use the following:

   ```
   puppet cert clean agent.example.net
   ```

   - On the agent, use the following:
   - On most platforms, use the following:

   ```
   find /etc/puppetlabs/puppet/ssl -name
   agent.example.net.pem -delete
   ```

   - On Windows, use the following:

   ```
   del "/etc/puppetlabs/puppet/ssl/agent.example.net.pem"
   /f
   puppet agent -t
   Exiting; failed to retrieve certificate and waitforcert
   is disabled
   ```

4. Once you perform the cleanup operation on the master, as advised in the preceding output, and remove the indicated file from the agent machine, the agent will be able to successfully place its new CSR:

```
root@puppetmaster# puppet cert clean agent
Notice: Revoked certificate with serial 18
Notice: Removing file Puppet::SSL::Certificate agent at
'/etc/puppetlabs/ puppet/ssl/ca/signed/agent.pem'
Notice: Removing file Puppet::SSL::Certificate agent at
'/etc/puppetlabs/ puppet/ssl/certs/agent.pem'
```

The rest of the process is identical to the original certificate creation. The agent uploads its CSR to the master, where the certificate is created through the puppet cert sign command.

Running the agent from cron

There is an alternative way to operate the agent. We covered starting one long-running `puppet agent` process that does its work in set intervals and then goes back to sleep. However, it is also possible to have cron launch a discrete agent process in the same interval. This agent will contact the master once, run the received catalog, and then terminate. This has several advantages, as follows:

- The agent operating system saves resources
- The interval is precise and not subject to skew (when running the background agent, deviations result from the time that elapses during the catalog run), and distributed interval skew can lead to thundering herd effects
- Any agent crash or an inadvertent termination is not fatal

Setting Puppet to run the agent from cron is also very easy to do with Puppet! You can use a manifest like the following:

```
service { 'puppet': enable => false, }
cron { 'puppet-agent-run':
  user    => 'root',
  command => 'puppet agent --no-daemonize --onetime --logdest=syslog',
  minute  => fqdn_rand(60),
  hour    => absent,
}
```

The `fqdn_rand` function computes a distinct minute for each of your agents. Setting the `hour` property to `absent` means that the job should run every hour.

Performance optimizations

Operating a Puppet master gives you numerous benefits over just using `puppet apply` on all your machines. This comes at a cost, of course. The master and agents form a server/client relation, and, as with most such constructs, the server can become the bottleneck.

The good news is that the Puppet agent is a fat client. The major share of the work inspecting file contents, interfacing with the package-management subsystem, services subsystem, and much more is done by the agent. The master only has to compile manifests and build catalogs from them. This becomes increasingly complex as you hand over more control to Puppet.

There is one more task your master is responsible for. Many of your manifests will contain file resources that rely on prepared content:

```
file { '/usr/local/etc/my_app.ini':
  ensure => file,
  owner  => 'root',
  group  => 'root',
  source =>
  'puppet:///modules/my_app/usr/local/etc/my_app.ini',
}
```

The `source` parameter with a URL value indicates that the file has been pregenerated and placed in a module on the Puppet master (more on modules in `Chapter 5`, *Combining Classes, Configuration Files, and Extensions into Modules*). The agent will compare the local file with the master's copy (by checksum) and download the canonical version, if required. The comparison is a frequent occurrence in most agent runs; you will make Puppet manage a lot of files. The master does not need a lot of resources to make this happen, but it *will* hinder fluent agent operation if the master gets congested.

This can happen for any combination of the following reasons:

- The total number of agents is too large
- The agents check in too frequently
- The manifests are too complex
- The Puppet server is not tuned adequately
- The master's hardware resources are insufficient

There are ways to scale your master operation via load balancing, but these are not covered in this book.

> Puppet Labs have some documentation on a few advanced approaches at `https://docs.puppetlabs.com/guides/scaling_multiple_masters.html`.

Tuning puppetserver

The puppetserver is a great way to run the master service. It is simple to set up and maintain, and it also has great performance during the operation. Starting up can take a little while to initialize everything to that end.

There are only a few customizable settings that can impact performance. Seeing as puppetserver runs in the JVM, the most important tuning approach is to scale the heap. A small heap will increase the overhead for garbage collection. Therefore, you should use the -Xmx and -Xms Java options to allow the JVM to use large parts of your available memory for the aforementioned heap.

On Debian, these settings are found in /etc/default/puppetserver. It is sensible to pass the same value to both. A dynamic heap has little benefit because you cannot safely use any saved memory.

For proper puppetserver functionality, it is recommended that you have 4 GB of RAM available.

Completing the stack with PuppetDB

PuppetDB is a specialized database REST API designed to interact with the Puppet master. It mainly comprises a PostgreSQL backend with an API wrapper. The latter was written in Clojure and runs in yet another JVM.

PuppetDB aids the master's secondary task of storing reports and other agent data. It is also necessary for some specific manifest compiler functionality. This is covered in Chapter 6, *The Puppet Beginners Advanced Parts*.

The best way to set up and configure PuppetDB is actually Puppet itself. Since the necessary tools have not yet been introduced, we will postpone this step until Chapter 6, *The Puppet Beginners Advanced Parts*. This is not a problem, because PuppetDB is not essential for basic master operation.

Nevertheless, after finishing this chapter, you should include PuppetDB into any new master setup because it allows for advanced reporting and introspection.

The Puppet CA

Among the most frustrating issues, especially for new users, are problems with the agent's SSL handshake. Such errors are especially troublesome because Puppet cannot always offer very helpful analysis in its logs - the problems occur in the SSL library functions, and the application cannot examine the circumstances.

The online documentation at Puppet Labs has a **troubleshooting** section that also has some advice concerning SSL-related issues at
https://docs.puppetlabs.com/guides/troubleshooting.html.

Consider the following output for the --test command:

```
root@agent# puppet agent --test
Warning: Unable to fetch my node definition, but the agent run will
continue:
Warning: SSL_connect returned=1 errno=0 state=unknown state: certificate
verify failed: [CRL is not yet valid for /CN=Puppet CA: puppet.example.net]
```

The agent opines that the CRL it receives from the master is not yet valid. Errors such as these can happen whenever the agent's clock gets reset to a very early date. This can also result from a slight clock skew, when the CRL has recently been updated through a revocation action on the master. If the system clock on the agent machine returns a time far in the future, it will consider certificates to be expired.

These clock-related issues are best avoided by running an ntp service on all Puppet agents and masters.

Errors will generally result if the data in the agent's `$ssldir` becomes inconsistent. This can happen when the agent interacts with an alternate master (a testing instance, for example). The first piece of advice you will most likely receive when asking the community what to do about such problems is to create a new agent certificate from scratch. This works as described in the *The agent's life cycle* section:

- Remove all the SSL data from the agent machine
- Revoke and remove the certificate from the master using `puppet cert clean`
- Request and sign a new certificate

Before you start the recovery procedure, make sure that you are logged in to the afflicted agent machine and not the master. Losing the master's SSL data will make it necessary to recreate your complete SSL infrastructure.

This approach will indeed remedy most issues. Be careful not to leave any old files in the relevant location on the agent machine. If the problems persist, a more involved solution is required. The openssl command-line tool is helpful to analyze the certificates and related files. The details of such an analysis are beyond the scope of this book, though.

Summary

You can now set up your own Puppet master, using the sophisticated puppetserver solution. You have successfully signed the certificate for a Puppet agent and can revoke certificates, if required. Using the `node` blocks in the master manifest, you can describe individual manifests for each distinct agent. Finally, you learned about some things that can go wrong with the SSL-based authentication.

In `Chapter 3`, *A Peek into the Ruby Part of Puppet - Facts, Types, and Providers*, we will take a look at the inner workings of Puppet in order to give you an understanding of how the Puppet agent adapts to its environment. You will also learn how the agent provides feedback to the master, allowing you to create flexible manifests that fit different needs.

3
A Peek into the Ruby Part of Puppet - Facts, Types, and Providers

So far in this book, you have primarily done practical things - writing manifests, setting up a master, assigning agents, signing certificates, and so forth. Before you are introduced to the missing language concepts that you will need to use Puppet effectively for bigger projects, there is some background that we should cover. Don't worry, it won't be all dry theory - most of the important parts of Puppet are relevant to your daily business.

The topics of this chapter have been hinted at earlier; Chapter 1, *Writing Your First Manifests*, contained a brief description of the type and provider. This and some adjacent topics will be thoroughly explored in the sections collecting system information with Facter, understanding the type system, and command execution control with providers.

Putting it all together - collecting system information with Facter

Configuration management is quite a dynamic problem. In other words, the systems that need configuration are mostly moving targets. In some situations, system administrators or operators get lucky and work with large quantities of 100 percent uniform hardware and software. In most cases, however, the landscape of servers and other computing nodes is rather heterogeneous, at least in subtle ways. Even in unified networks, there are likely multiple generations of machines or operating systems, with smaller or larger differences required for their respective configurations.

For example, a common task for Puppet is to handle the configuration of system monitoring. Your business logic will likely dictate warning thresholds for gauges such as the system load value. However, those thresholds can rarely be static. On a two-processor virtual machine, a system load of 10 represents a crippling overload, while the same value can be absolutely acceptable for a busy DBMS server that has cutting edge hardware of the largest dimensions.

Another important factor can be software platforms. Your infrastructure might span multiple distributions of Linux or alternate operating systems, such as BSD, Solaris, or Windows, each with different ways of handling certain scenarios. Imagine, for example, that you want Puppet to manage some content from the fstab file. On your rare Solaris system, you would have to make sure that Puppet targets the /etc/vfstab file instead of /etc/fstab.

It is usually not a good idea to interact directly with the fstab file in your manifest. This example will be rounded off in the section concerning providers.

Puppet strives to present you with a unified way of managing all your infrastructure. It therefore needs a means to allow your manifests to adapt to different kinds of circumstances on the agent machines. This includes their operating system, hardware layout, and many other details. Keep in mind that, generally, the manifests have to be compiled on the master machine.

There are several conceivable ways to implement a solution for this particular problem. A direct approach would be to use a language construct that allows the master to send a piece of shell script (or other code) to the agent and receive its output in return.

The following is pseudocode; however, there are no back tick expressions in the Puppet DSL:

```
if `grep -c ^processor /proc/cpuinfo` > 2 {
  $load_warning = 4
}
else {
  $load_warning = 2
}
```

This solution would be powerful but expensive. The master would need to call back to the agent whenever the compilation process encountered such an expression. Writing manifests that were able to cope with such a command returning an error code would be strenuous, and Puppet would likely end up resembling a quirky scripting engine.

Puppet uses a different approach. It relies on a secondary system called Facter, which has the sole purpose of examining the machine on which it is run. It serves a list of well-known variable names and values, all according to the system on which it runs. For example, an actual Puppet manifest that needs to form a condition upon the number of processors on the agent will use this expression:

```
if $::processors['count'] > 4 { ... }
```

Facter's variables are called **facts**, and `processors` is one such fact. With Facter version 3 or later, most data will be gathered and presented as structured facts (JSON). In the example, we accessed the `'count'` element from 'processors' data. The older key-value pairs are still available. The fact values are gathered by the agent and sent to the master, who will use these facts to compile a catalog. All fact names are available in the manifests as variables.

> Facts are also available to manifests that are used with `puppet apply`, of course. You can test this very simply with the following:
> ```
> puppet apply -e 'notify { "I am ${::networking['fqdn']}
> and have ${::processors['count']} CPUs": }'
> ```

Accessing and using fact values

You have already seen the use of the `processors` fact in an example. In the manifest, each fact value is available as a global variable value. That is why you can just use the `::processors` expression where you need it.

You will often see conventional uses such as `$::processors['count']` or `$::networking['ip']`. Prefixing the fact name with double colons is highly recommended. The official style guide at `https://docs.puppetlabs.com/guides/style_guide.html#namespacing-variables` recommends this. The prefix indicates that you are referring to a variable delivered from Facter. Facter variables are put into the Puppet master's top scope.

Some helpful facts have already been mentioned. The `processors` fact might play a role for your configuration. When configuring some services, you will want to use the machine's `networking ['ip']` value in a configuration file or as an argument value:

```
file { '/etc/mysql/conf.d/bind-address':
  ensure  => 'file',
  mode    => '0644',
  content => "[mysqld]\nbind-address=${::networking['ip']}\n",
}
```

Apart from the hostname, your manifest can also make use of the **Fully Qualified Domain Name (FQDN)** of the agent machine.

The agent will use the value of its `fqdn` fact as the name of its certificate (`clientcert`) by default. The master receives both these values. Note that the agent can override the `fqdn` value of any name, whereas the `clientcert` value is tied to the signed certificate that the agent uses. Sometimes, you will want the master to pass sensitive information to individual nodes. The manifest must identify the agent by its `clientcert` fact and never use `fqdn` or `hostname` instead, for the reason mentioned. An example is shown in the following code:

```
file { '/etc/my-secret':
  ensure => 'file',
  mode    => '0600',
  owner   => 'root',
  source =>
  "puppet:///modules/secrets/${::clientcert}/key",
}
```

There is a whole group of facts that are used to describe the operating system. Each fact is useful in different situations. The `os['name']` fact takes values such as `Debian` or `CentOS`:

```
if $::os['name'] != 'Ubuntu' {
  package { 'avahi-daemon':
    ensure => absent
  }
}
```

If your manifest will behave identically on RHEL, CentOS, and Fedora (but not on Debian and Ubuntu), you should make use of the `osfamily` fact instead:

```
if $::os['family'] == 'RedHat' {
  $kernel_package = 'kernel'
}
```

The `os['release']['full']` fact allows you to tailor your manifests to the different versions of your OS:

```
if $::so['name'] == 'Debian' {
  if versioncmp($::os['release']['full'], '7.0') >= 0 {
    $ssh_ecdsa_support = true
  }
}
```

Facts such as mac address, the different SSH host keys, fingerprints, and others make it easy to use Puppet for keeping an inventory of your hardware. There are a slew of other useful facts. Of course, the collection will not suit every possible need of every user out there. That is why Facter comes readily extendible.

Extending Facter with custom facts

Technically, nothing is stopping you from adding your own fact code right next to the core facts, either by maintaining your own Facter package, or even by deploying the Ruby code files to your agents directly through Puppet management. However, Puppet offers a much more convenient alternative in the form of custom facts.

We have still not covered Puppet modules yet. They will be thoroughly introduced in Chapter 5, *Combining Classes, Configuration Files, and Extensions into Modules*. For now, just create a Ruby file at
`/etc/puppetlabs/code/environments/production/modules/hello_world/lib/facter/hello.rb` on the master machine. Puppet will recognize this as a custom fact of the name, `hello`. (For Puppet 3 or older versions, the path should be
`/etc/puppet/modules/hello_world/lib/facter/hello.rb`.)

The inner workings of Facter are very straightforward and goal oriented. There is one block of Ruby code for each fact, and the return value of the block becomes the fact value. Many facts are self-sufficient, but others will rely on the values of one or more basic facts. For example, the method to determine the IP address(es) of the local machine is highly dependent upon the operating system.

The `hello` fact is very simple, though:

```
Facter.add(:hello) do
  setcode { "Hello, world!" }
end
```

The return value of the `setcode` block is the string `Hello, world!`, and you can use this fact as `$::hello` in a Puppet manifest.

Before Facter version 2.0, each fact had a string value. If a code block returns another value, such as an array or hash, Facter 1.x will convert it to a string. The result is not useful in many cases. For this historic reason, there are facts such as `ipaddress_eth0` and `ipaddress_lo` instead of (or in addition to) a proper hash structure with interface names and addresses.

It is important for the `pluginsync` option to be enabled on the agent side. This has been the default for a long time and should not require any customization. The agent will synchronize all custom facts whenever checking in to the master. They are permanently available on the agent machine after that. You can then retrieve the `hello` fact from the command line using the following line:

```
# puppet facts | grep hello
```

Just by invoking the following command without an argument, you can request a list of all fact names and values.

```
# puppet facts
```

There is also a `facter` command. It does roughly the same as puppet facts, but will only show built-in facts, not your custom facts.

> In Puppet 3 and earlier, there was no puppet facts subcommand. You had to rely on the Facter CLI (from Facter version 2.x or older) and call `facter` `-p`, to include custom facts. Some versions of Facter 3.0 removed this parameter; newer versions support it again.

This book will not cover all aspects of Facter's API, but there is one facility that is quite essential. Many of your custom facts will only be useful on Unix-like systems, and others will only be useful on your Windows boxes. You can retrieve such facts using a construct the same as the following:

```
if Facter.value(:kernel) != "windows"
  nil
else
  # actual fact code here
end
```

This would be quite tedious and repetitive, though. Instead, you can invoke the `confine` method within the `Facter.add(name) { ... }` block:

```
Facter.add(:msvs_version) do
  confine :kernel => :windows
  setcode do
    # ...
  end
end
```

You can confine a fact to several alternative values as well:

```
confine :kernel => [ :linux, :sunos ]
```

Finally, if a fact does make sense in different circumstances, but requires drastically different code in each respective case, you can add the same fact several times, each with a different set of `confine` values. Core facts such as `ipaddress` use this often:

```
Facter.add(:ipaddress) do
  confine :kernel => :linux
  ...
end
Facter.add(:ipaddress) do
  confine :kernel => %w{FreeBSD OpenBSD Darwin DragonFly}
  ...
end
...
```

You can confine facts based on any combination of other facts, not just `kernel`. It is a very popular choice though. The `operatingsystem` or `osfamily` facts can be more appropriate in certain situations. Technically, you can even confine some of your facts to certain `processorcount` values, and so forth.

Simplifying things using external facts

If writing and maintaining Ruby code is not desirable in your team for any reason, you might prefer to use an alternative that allows shell scripts, or really any kind of programming language, or even static data with no programming involved at all. Facter allows this in the form of **external facts**.

Creating an external fact is similar to the process used for regular custom facts, with the following distinctions:

- External facts are produced by standalone executables or files with static data, which the agent must find in `/etc/puppetlabs/facter/facts.d/`
- The data is not just a string value, but an arbitrary number of `key=value` pairs instead

The data need not use the `ini` file notation style; the key/value pairs can also be in the YAML or JSON format. The following external facts hold the same data:

```
# site-facts.txt
workgroup='CT4Site2'
domain_psk='nm56DxLp%'
```

The facts can be written in the YAML format in the following way:

```
# site-facts.yaml
workgroup: 'CT4Site2'
domain_psk: 'nm56DxLp%'
```

In the JSON format, facts can be written as follows:

```
# site-facts.json
{ 'workgroup': 'CT4Site2', 'domain_psk': 'nm56DxLp%' }
```

The deployment of the external facts works simply through `file` resources in your Puppet manifest:

```
file { '/etc/puppetlabs/facter/facts.d/site-facts.yaml':
  ensure => 'file',
  source => 'puppet:///...',
}
```

With newer versions of Puppet and Facter, external facts will be automatically synchronized, just as custom facts, if they are found in `facts.d/*` in any module (for example, `/etc/puppetlabs/code/environments/production/modules/hello_world/facts.d/hello.sh`). This is not only more convenient, but has a large benefit: when Puppet must fetch an external fact through a `file` resource instead, as its fact value(s) are not available while the catalog is being compiled. The `pluginsync` mechanism, on the other hand, makes sure that all synced facts are available before manifest compilation starts.

When facts are not static and cannot be placed in a `txt` or `YAML` file, you can make the file executable and add a shebang instead. It will usually be a shell script, but the implementation is of no consequence; it is just important that properly formatted data is written to the standard output. You can simplify the `hello` fact this way, in `/etc/puppetlabs/code/environments/production/modules/hello_world/facts.d/hello.sh`:

```
#!/bin/sh
echo hello=Hello, world\!
```

For executable facts, the `ini` styled `key=value` format is the only supported format. YAML or JSON are not eligible in this context.

Facter 2 introduced structured facts. Structured facts return an array or a hash. In older Puppet versions (prior to 3.4), structured facts have to be enabled in `puppet.conf` by setting `stringify_facts` to false. This is the default setting for Puppet 4.0 and later versions.

Goals of Facter

The whole structure and philosophy of Facter serves the goal of allowing for platform-agnostic usage and development. The same collection of facts (roughly) is available on all supported platforms. This allows Puppet users to keep a coherent development style throughout their manifests for all those different systems.

Facter forms a layer of abstraction over the characteristics of both hardware and software. It is an important piece of Puppet's platform-independent architecture. Another feature that was mentioned before is the type and provider subsystem. Types and providers are explored in greater detail in the following sections.

Understanding the type system

Being one of the cornerstones of the Puppet model, resources were introduced quite early in `Chapter 1`, *Writing Your First Manifests*. Remember how each resource represents a piece of state on the agent system. It has a resource type, a name (or a title), and a list of attributes. An attribute can either be `property` or `parameter`. Between the two of them, properties represent distinct pieces of state, and parameters merely influence Puppet's actions upon the `property` values.

Let's examine resource types in more detail and understand their inner workings. This is not only important when extending Puppet with resource types of your own (which will be demonstrated in `Chapter 5`, *Combining Classes, Configuration Files, and Extensions into Modules*). It also helps you anticipate the action that Puppet will take, given your manifest, and get a better understanding of both the master and the agent.

First, we take a closer look at the operational structure of Puppet, with its pieces and phases. The agent performs all its work in discreet **transactions**. A transaction is started under any of the following circumstances:

- The background agent process activates and checks in to the master
- An agent process is started with the `--onetime` or `--test` options
- A local manifest is compiled using `puppet apply`

The transaction always passes several stages. They are as follows:

1. Gathering fact values to form the actual catalog request.
2. Receiving the compiled catalog from the master.
3. Prefetching of current resource states.
4. Validation of the catalog's content.
5. Synchronization of the system with the `property` values from the catalog.

Facter was explained in the previous section. The resource types become important during compilation and then throughout the rest of the agent transaction. The master loads all resource types to perform some basic checking; it basically makes sure that the types of resources it finds in the manifests do exist and that the attribute names fit the respective type.

The resource type's life cycle on the agent side

Once the compilation has succeeded, the master hands out the catalog and the agent enters the catalog validation phase. Each resource type can define some Ruby methods that ensure that the passed values make sense. This happens on two levels of granularity: Each attribute can validate its input value, and then the resource as a whole can be checked for consistency.

One example of attribute value validation can be found in the `ssh_authorized_key` resource type. A resource of this type fails if its `key` value contains a whitespace character because SSH keys cannot comprise multiple strings.

Validation of whole resources happens with the `cron` type, for example. It makes sure that the `time` fields make sense together. The following resource would not pass, because special times, such as `midgnight`, cannot be combined with numeric fields:

```
cron { 'invalid-resource':
  command => 'apt-get update',
  special => 'midnight',
  weekday => [ '2', '5' ],
}
```

Another task during this phase is the transformation of input values to more suitable internal representations. The resource type code refers to this as a `munge` action. Typical examples of munging are the removal of leading and trailing whitespace from string values, or the conversion of array values to an appropriate string format-this can be a comma-separated list, but for search paths, the separator should be a colon instead. Other kinds of values will use different representations.

Next up is the prefetching phase. Some resource types allow the agent to create an internal list of resource instances that are present on the system. These types are referred to as being enumerable types. For example, this is possible (and makes sense) for installed packages-Puppet can just invoke the package manager to produce the list. For other types, such as `file`, this would not be prudent. Creating a list of all reachable paths in the whole filesystem can be arbitrarily expensive, depending on the system on which the agent is running.

The prefetching can be simulated by running `puppet resource <resource type> <title>` on the command line as follows:

```
# puppet resource user root
  user { 'root':
    ensure              => 'present',
    comment             => 'root',
    gid                 => '0',
    home                => '/root',
    password            => '$6$17[...]o.rLdk/9MZANEGt/',
    password_max_age    => '99999',
    password_min_age    => '0',
    shell               => '/bin/bash',
    uid                 => '0',
  }
```

Finally, the agent starts walking through its internal graph of interdependent resources. Each resource is brought in sync, if necessary. This happens separately for each individual property, for the most part.

The `ensure` property, for types that support it, is a notable exception. It is expected to manage all other properties on its own; when a resource is changed from `absent` to `present` through its `ensure` property (in other words, the resource is getting newly created), this action should bring all other properties in sync as well.

There are some notable aspects of the whole agent process. For one, attributes are handled independently. Each can define its own methods for the different phases. There are quite a number of hooks, which allow a resource type author to add a lot of flexibility to the model.

For aspiring type authors, skimming through the core types can be quite inspirational. You will be familiar with many attributes; using them in your manifests and studying their hooks will offer quite some insight.

It is also worth noting that the whole validation process is performed by the agent, not the master. This is beneficial in terms of performance. The master saves a lot of work, which gets distributed to the network of agents (which scales with your needs automatically).

Command execution control with providers

At the start of this chapter, you learned about Facter and how it works as a layer of abstraction over the supported platforms. This unified information base is one of Puppet's most important means of achieving its goal of operating system independence. Another one is the DSL, of course. Finally, Puppet also needs a method to transparently adapt its behavior to the respective platform on which each agent runs.

In other words, depending on the characteristics of the computing environment, the agent needs to switch between different implementations for its resources. This is not unlike object oriented programming-the type system provides a unified interface, not unlike an abstract base class. The programmer need not worry what specific class is being referenced, as long as it correctly implements all the required methods. In this analogy, Puppet's providers are the concrete classes that implement the abstract interface.

For a practical example, look at package management. Different flavors of Unix-like operating systems have their own implementation. The most prevalent Puppet platforms use apt and yum, respectively, but can (and sometimes must) also manage their packages through dpkg and rpm. Other platforms use tools such as emerge, zypper, fink, and a slew of other things. There are even packages that exist apart from the operating system software base, handled through gem, pip, and other language-specific package management tools. For each of these management tools, there is a provider for the package type.

Many of these tools allow the same set of operations-installing and uninstalling a package, and updating a package to a specific version. However, the latter is not universally possible. For example, dpkg can only ever install the local package that is specified on the command line, with no other version to choose.

There are also some distinct features that are unique to specific tools, or are supported by only a few. Some management systems can hold packages at specific versions. Some use different states for uninstalled versus purged packages. Some have a concept of virtual packages. The list of examples can go on and on.

Because of this potential diversity (which is not limited to package management systems), Puppet providers can opt for **features**. The set of features is resource-type specific. All providers for a type can support one or more of the same group of features. For the package type, there are features such as versionable, purgeable, holdable, and so forth. You can set ensure => purged on any package resource as so:

```
package { 'haproxy':
  ensure => 'purged'
}
```

However, if you are managing the HAproxy package through rpm, Puppet will fail to make any sense of it because rpm has no notion of a purged state, and therefore, the purgeable feature is missing from the rpm provider. Trying to use an unsupported feature will usually produce an error message. Some attributes, such as install_options, might just result in a warning by Puppet instead.

The official documentation on the Puppet Labs website holds a complete list of the core resource types and all their built-in providers, along with the respective feature matrices. It is very easy to find suitable providers and their capabilities. The documentation can be found at https://docs. puppetlabs.com/references/latest/type.html.

Resource types with generic providers

There are some resource types that use no providers, but they are rare among the core types. Most of the interesting management tasks that Puppet makes easy just work differently among operating systems, and providers enable this in a most elegant fashion.

Even for straightforward tasks that are the same on all platforms, there might be a provider. For example, there is a `host` type to manage entries in the `/etc/hosts` file. Its syntax is universal, so the code can technically just be implemented in the type. However, there are actual abstract base classes for certain kinds of providers in the Puppet code base. One of them makes it very easy to build providers that edit files, if those files consist of single-line records with ordered fields. Therefore, it makes sense to implement a provider for the `host` type and base it on this provider class.

For the curious, this is what a host resource looks like:

```
host { 'puppet':
    ip             => '10.144.12.100',
    host_aliases => [ 'puppet.example.net', 'master' ],
}
```

Summarizing types and providers

Puppet's resource types and their providers work together to form a solid abstraction layer over software configuration details. The type system is an extendable basis for Puppet's powerful DSL. It forms an elaborate interface for the polymorphous provider layer.

The providers flexibly implement the actual management actions that Puppet is supposed to perform. They map the necessary synchronization steps to commands and system interactions. Many providers cannot satisfy every nuance that the resource type models. The feature system takes care of these disparities in a transparent fashion.

Putting it all together

Reading this far, you might have gotten the impression that this chapter is a rather odd mix of topics. While types and providers do belong closely together, the whole introduction to Facter might seem out of place in this context. However, this is deceptive; facts do play a vital role in the type/provider structure. They are essential for Puppet to make good choices between the providers.

Let's look at an example from the *Extending Facter with custom facts* section once more. It was about `fstab` entries and the difference of Solaris, which uses `/etc/vfstab` instead of `/etc/fstab`. That section suggested a manifest that adapts according to a fact value. As you have learned, Puppet has a resource type to manage `fstab` content: the `mount` type. However, for the small deviation of a different file path, there is no dedicated `mount` provider for Solaris. There is actually just one provider for all platforms, but on Solaris, it behaves differently. It does this by resolving Facter's `os['family']` value. The following code example was adapted from the actual provider code:

```
case Facter.value(:os['family'])
when"Solaris"
  fstab = "/etc/vfstab"
else
  fstab = "/etc/fstab"
end
```

In other cases, however, Puppet should use thoroughly different providers on different platforms. Package management is a classic example. On a Red Hat-like platform, you will want Puppet to use the `yum` provider in virtually all cases. It can be sensible to use `rpm`, and even `apt` might be available. However, if you tell Puppet to make sure a package is installed, you expect it to install it using `yum`, if necessary.

This is obviously a common theme. Certain management tasks need to be performed in different environments, with very different toolchains. In such cases, it is quite clear which provider would be best suited. To make this happen, a provider can declare itself the default if a condition is met. In the case of `yum`, it is the following:

```
defaultfor :os['name'] => [:fedora, :centos, :redhat]
```

The conditions are based around fact values. If the `operatingsystem` value for a given agent is among the listed, `yum` will consider itself the default package provider.

The operating system and os family facts are the most popular choices for such queries in providers, but any fact is eligible.

In addition to marking themselves as default, there is more filtering of providers that rely on fact values. Providers can also confine themselves to certain combinations of values. For example, the `yum` alternative, `zypper`, confines itself to SUSE Linux distributions:

```
confine :os['name'] => [:suse, :sles, :sled, :opensuse]
```

This provider method works just as the `confine` method in Facter, which was discussed earlier in this chapter. The provider will not even be seen as valid if the respective facts on the agent machine have none of the white-listed values.

 If you find yourself looking through code for some core providers, you will notice confinement (and even the declaration of default providers) on feature values, although there is no Facter fact of that name. These features are not related to provider features either. They are from another layer of introspection similar to Facter, but hardcoded into the Puppet agent. These agent features are a number of flags that identify some system properties that need not be made available to manifests in the form of facts. For example, the `posix` provider for the `exec` type becomes the default in the presence of the corresponding feature: `defaultfor :feature => :posix`

You will find that some providers forgo the `confine` method altogether, as it is not mandatory for correct agent operation. Puppet will also identify unsuitable providers when looking for their necessary operating system commands. For example, the `pw` provider for certain BSD flavors does not bother with a `confine` statement. It only declares its one required command:

```
commands :pw => "pw"
```

Agents that find no `pw` binary in their search path will not try and use this provider at all.

This concludes the little tour of the inner workings of types and providers with the help of Facter. For a complete example of building a provider for a type, and using the internal tools that you have now learned about, you can refer to `Chapter 5`, *Combining Classes, Configuration Files, and Extensions into Modules*.

Summary

Puppet gathers information about all agent systems using Facter. The information base consists of a large number of independent bits, called facts. Manifests can query the values of those facts to adapt to the respective agents that trigger their compilation. Puppet also uses facts to choose among providers, the work horses that make the abstract resource types functional across the wide range of supported platforms.

The resource types not only completely define the interface that Puppet exposes in the DSL, they also take care of all the validation of input values, transformations that must be performed before handing values to the providers, and other related tasks.

The providers encapsulate all knowledge of actual operating systems and their respective toolchains. They implement the functionality that the resource types describe. The Puppet model's configurations apply to platforms, which vary from one another, so not every facet of every resource type can make sense for all agents. By exposing only the supported features, a provider can express such limitations.

After this in-depth look at the internal details, let's tackle more practical concerns again. The following chapters will cover the tools needed to build complex and advanced manifests of all scales.

4
Combining Resources in Classes and Defined Types

At this point, you have already performed some production-grade tasks with Puppet. You learned how to write standalone manifests and then invoke `puppet apply` to put them to use. While setting up your first Puppet master and agent, you created a simple example for a node manifest on the master. In a `node '<hostname>'` block, you created the equivalent of a manifest file. This way, the Puppet master used just this manifest for the specified agent node.

While this is all useful and essentially important, it will obviously not suffice for daily business. By working with `node` blocks that contain sets of resources, you will end up performing lots of copy and paste operations for similar nodes, and the whole construct will become unwieldy very quickly. This is an unnatural approach to developing Puppet manifests. Despite the great differences to many other languages that you might be familiar with, the Puppet DSL is a programming language. Building manifests merely from `node` blocks and resources would be the same as writing C with no functions except `main`, or Ruby without any classes of your own.

The manifests that you can write with the means that are already at your disposal are not flat, you learned about common control structures such as `if` and `case`. Your manifests can use these to adapt to various circumstances on the agent by querying the values of Facter facts and branching in accordance with the results.

However, these constructs should be complemented by the language tools to create reusable units of manifest code, similar to functions or methods in procedural languages. This chapter introduces these concepts through the following topics:

- Introducing classes and defined types
- Design patterns
- The dynamic aspect of defined types
- Ordering and events among classes
- Making classes more flexible through parameters

Introducing classes and defined types

Puppet's equivalents to methods or functions are twofold: there are **classes** on one hand and defined types (also just referred to as defines) on the other.

> You will find that the function analogy is a bit weak for classes, but fits defined types quite well.

They are similar at first glance, in that they both hold a chunk of reusable Puppet DSL code. There are big differences in the way each is used though. Let's take a look at classes first.

Defining and declaring classes

A Puppet class can be considered to be a container containing collections of Puppet resource declarations. It is created once (class definition) and used by all nodes that need to make use of the prepared functionality. Each class represents a well-known subset of a system's configuration, such as `ntp`, `nginx`, and `ssh`.

For example, a classic use `case` is a class that installs the Apache web server and applies some basic settings. This class will look the same as the following:

```
class apache {
  package { 'apache2':
    ensure => present,
  }
  file { '/etc/apache2/apache2.conf':
    ensure => 'file',
    source =>
    'puppet:///modules/apache/etc/apache2/apache2.conf',
```

```
  }
  service { 'apache2':
    ensure    => running,
    enable    => true,
    subscribe => File['/etc/apache2/apache2.conf',
  }
}
```

All web server nodes will make use of this class. To this end, their manifests need to contain a simple statement:

```
include apache
```

This is referred to as including a class, or declaring it. If your `apache` class is powerful enough to do all that is needed, this line might fully comprise a `node` block's content:

```
node 'webserver01' {
  include apache
}
```

 In your own setup, you will probably not write your own Apache class. You can use open source classes that are available through Puppet modules. `Chapter 5`, *Combining Classes, Configuration Files, and Extensions into Modules*, will give you all the details.

This concludes our tour of classes in a nutshell. There is yet more to discuss, of course, but let's take a look at defined types before that.

Creating and using defined types

A defined type can be regarded as a new resource type which makes use of existing resource types. This is useful when you have repeating instances of existing resource types, as you can wrap them in a defined type. As a class, it consists mainly of a body containing the manifest code. However, a defined type takes arguments and makes their values available in its body as local variables.

Here is another typical example of a defined type, the Apache virtual host configuration:

```
define virtual_host(
  String $content,
  String[3,3] $priority = '050'
) {
  file { "/etc/apache2/sites-available/${name}":
    ensure  => 'file',
    owner   => 'root',
```

```
    group     => 'root',
    mode      => '0644',
    content => $content
  }
  file { "/etc/apache2/sites-enabled/${priority}-${name}":
    ensure => 'link',
    target => "../sites-available/${name}";
  }
}
```

 Data types such as String have been available since Puppet 4. In Puppet 3 and earlier, you would have just skipped these; all variables used to be untyped.

This code might still seem pretty cryptic. It will become clearer in the context of how it is actually used from other places in your manifest; the following code shows you how:

```
virtual_host { 'example.net':
  content => file('apache/vhosts/example.net')
}
virtual_host{ 'fallback':
  priority => '999',
  content  => file('apache/vhosts/fallback')
}
```

This is why the construct is called a defined type; you can now place what appear to be resources in your manifest, but you really call your own manifest code construct.

When declaring multiple resources of the same type, as in the preceding code, you can do so in a single block and separate them with a semicolon:

```
virtual_host {
  'example.net':
    content  => 'foo';
  'fallback':
    priority => '999',
    content  => ...,
}
```

 The official style guide forbids this syntax, but it can make manifests more readable and maintainable in some cases.

The `virtual_host` type takes two arguments: the `content` argument is mandatory as it has no default value and is used verbatim in the configuration file resource. Puppet will synchronize that file's content to what is specified in the manifest. The `priority` argument is optional and its value becomes the file name prefix. If omitted, the respective virtual host definition uses the default priority of `050`.

Both parameters of this example type are of the `String` type. For details about Puppet's variable type system, see `Chapter 5`, *Combining Classes, Configuration Files, and Extensions into Modules*. It suffices to say that you can restrict parameters to certain value types. This is optional, however. You can omit the type name, and Puppet will accept any value for the parameter in question.

Also, each defined type can implicitly refer to the name (or title) by which it was called. In other words, each instance that you define gets a name, and you can access it through the `$name` or `$title` variable.

There are a few other *magic* variables that are available in the body of a defined type. If a resource of the defined type is declared with a metaparameter such as `require => ...`, its value can be accessed through the `$require` variable in the body. The variable value remains empty if the metaparameter is not used. This works for metaparameters, such as `before`, `notify`, and all the others, but you will probably never need to make use of this. The metaparameters automatically do the right thing.

Understanding and leveraging the differences

The respective purposes of Puppet's class and defined type are very specific and they usually don't overlap.

The class declares resources and properties that are in some way centric to the system. A class is a finalized description of one, or sometimes more, aspect of your system as a whole. Whatever the class represents, it can only ever exist in one form; to Puppet, each class is implicitly a singleton, a fixed set of information that either applies to your system (the class is included), or not.

The typical resources you will encapsulate in a class for convenient inclusion in a manifest are as follows:

- One or more packages that should be installed (or removed)
- A specific configuration file in /etc
- A common directory, needed to store scripts or configs for many subsystems
- Cron jobs that should be mostly identical on all applicable systems

The define is used for all things that exist in multiple instances. All aspects that appear in varying quantities in your system can possibly be modeled using this language construct. In this regard, the define is very similar to the full-fledged resource it mimics with its declaration syntax. Some of the typical contents of defined types are:

- Files in a conf.d style directory
- Entries in an easily parseable file such as /etc/hosts
- Apache virtual hosts
- Schemas in a database
- Rules in a firewall

The class's singleton nature is especially valuable because it prevents clashes in the form of multiple resource declarations. Remember that each resource must be unique to a catalog. For example, consider a second declaration of the Apache package:

```
package { 'apache2': }
```

This declaration can be anywhere in the manifest of one of your web servers (for example, right in the node block, next to include apache); this additional declaration will prevent the successful compilation of a catalog.

> The reason for the prevention of a successful compilation is that Puppet currently cannot make sure that both declarations represent the same target state, or can be merged to form a composite state. It is likely that multiple declarations of the same resource may conflict about the desired value of property (for example, one declaration might want to ensure that a package is absent, while the other needs it to be present). You want to see Puppet as a declarative description of your system configuration state.

The virtue of the class is that there can be an arbitrary number of `include` statements for the same class strewn throughout the manifest. Puppet will commit the class's contents to the catalog just once.

The uniqueness constraint for resources applies to defined types. No two instances of your own define can share the same name. Using a name twice or more produces a compiler error:

```
virtual_host { 'wordpress':
  content  => file(...),
  priority => '011',
}
virtual_host { 'wordpress':
  content  => '# Dummy vhost',
  priority => '600',
}
```

Design patterns

Your knowledge of classes and defined types is still rather academic. You have learned about their defining aspects and the syntax to use them, but we have yet to give you a feeling of how these concepts come to bear in different real-life scenarios.

The following sections will present an overview of what you can do with these language tools.

Writing comprehensive classes

Many classes are written to make Puppet perform momentous tasks on the agent platform. Of these, the Apache class is probably one of the more modest examples. You can conceive a class that can be included from any machine's manifest and make sure that the following conditions are met:

- The firewalling software is installed and configured with a default ruleset
- The malware detection software is installed
- Cron jobs run the scanners at set intervals
- The mailing subsystem is configured to make sure the cron jobs can deliver their output

There are two general ways you can go about the task of creating a class of this magnitude. It can either become what one might call a **monolithic** implementation, a class with a large body that comprises all resources that work together to form the desired security baseline. This approach has the benefit of precisely describing your infrastructure, but it lacks maintainability. On the other hand, you could aim for a **composite** design, with few resources (or none at all) in the class body, and a number of include statements for simpler classes instead. The functionality is compartmentalized, and the central class acts as a collector. This is the common best practice way in which Puppet module developers work.

We have not yet touched on the ability of classes to include other classes. That's because it's quite simple. The body of a class can comprise almost any manifest, and the include statement is no exception. Among the few things that cannot appear in a class are node blocks.

Adding some life to the descriptions, this is roughly what the respective classes will look like:

```
class monolithic_security {
  package { [ 'iptables', 'rkhunter', 'postfix' ]:
    ensure => 'installed';
  }
  cron { 'run-rkhunter':
    ...
  }
  file { '/etc/init.d/iptables-firewall':
    source => ...
    mode => 755
  }
  file { '/etc/postfix/main.cf':
    ensure => 'file',
    content => ...
  }
  service { [ 'postfix', 'iptables-firewall' ]:
    ensure => 'running',
    enable => true
  }
}
class divided_security {
  include iptables_firewall
  include rkhunter
  include postfix
}
```

When developing your own functional classes, you should not try to pick either of these extremes. Most classes will end up anywhere on the spectrum in between. The choice can be largely based on your personal preference. The technical implications are subtle, but these are the respective drawbacks:

- Consequently aiming for monolithic classes opens you up to resource clashes, because you take almost no advantage of the singleton nature of classes
- Splitting up classes too much can make it difficult to impose order and distribute refresh events, you can refer to the Combining classes, configuration files and extensions into Modules section later in this chapter

Neither of these aspects is of critical importance at most times. The case-by-case design choices will be based on each author's experience and preference. When in doubt, lean towards composite designs at first.

Writing component classes

There is another common use case for classes. Instead of filling a class with lots of aspects that work together to achieve a complex goal, you can also limit the class to a very specific purpose. Some classes will contain just one resource. The class wraps the resource, so to speak.

This is useful for resources that are needed in different contexts. By wrapping them away in a class, you can make sure that those contexts do not create multiple declarations of the same resource.

For example, the netcat package can be useful to firewall servers, but also to web application servers. There is probably a firewall class and an appserver class. Both declare the netcat package:

```
package { 'netcat':
  ensure => 'installed'
}
```

If any server ever has both roles (this might happen for budget reasons or in other unforeseen circumstances), it is a problem; when both the `firewall` and `appserver` classes are included, and the resulting manifest declares the `netcat` package twice. This is forbidden. To resolve this situation, the package resource can be wrapped in a `netcat` class, which is included by both the `firewall` and `appserver` classes:

```
class netcat {
  package { 'netcat':
    ensure => 'installed'
  }
}
```

Let's consider another typical example for component classes that ensures the presence of a common file path. Assume your IT policy requires all custom scripts and applications to be installed in `/opt/company/bin`. Many classes, such as `firewall` and `appserver` from the previous example, will need some relevant content there. Each class needs to make sure that the directories exist before a script can be deployed inside it. This will be implemented by including a component class that wraps the `file` resources of the `directory` tree:

```
class scripts_directory {
  file { [ '/opt/company/', '/opt/company/bin' ]:
    ensure => 'directory',
    owner  => 'root',
    group  => 'root',
    mode   => '0755',
  }
}
```

The component class is a pretty precise concept. However, as you have seen in the previous section about the more powerful classes, the whole range of possible class designs forms a fine-grained scale between the presented examples. All manifests you write will likely comprise more than a few classes. The best way to get a feeling for the best practices is to just go ahead and use classes to build the manifests you need.

> The terms **comprehensive** class and **component** class are not official Puppet language, and the community does not use them to communicate design practices. We chose them arbitrarily to describe the ideas we laid out in these sections. The same holds `true` for the descriptions of the use cases for defined types, which will be seen in the next sections.

Next, let's look at some uses for defined types.

Using defined types as resource wrappers

For all their apparent similarity to classes, defined types are used in different ways. For example, the component class was described as *wrapping a resource*. This is accurate in a very specific context, the wrapped resource is a singleton, and it can only appear in one form throughout the manifest.

When wrapping a resource in a defined type instead, you end up with a variation on the respective resource type. The manifest can contain an arbitrary number of instances of the defined type, and each will wrap a distinct resource.

For this to work, the name of the resource that is declared in the body of the defined type must be dynamically created. It is almost always the $name variable of the respective defined type instance, or a value derived from it.

Here is yet another typical example from the many manifests out there: most users who make use of Puppet's file serving capabilities will want to wrap the `file` type at some point so that the respective URL need not be typed for each file:

```
define module_file(String $module) {
  file { $title:
    source => "puppet:///modules/${module}/${title}"
  }
}
```

This makes it easy to get Puppet to sync files from the master to the agent. The master copy must be properly placed in the named modules on the master:

```
module_file { '/etc/ntpd.conf':
  module => 'ntp':
}
```

This resource will make Puppet retrieve the `ntp.conf` file from the `ntp` module. The preceding declaration is more concise and less redundant than the fully written file resource with the Puppet URL (especially for the large number of files you might need to synchronize), which would resemble the following:

```
file { '/etc/ntpd.conf':
  source => 'puppet:///modules/ntp/etc/ntpd.conf':
}
```

For a wrapper such as `module_file`, which will probably be used very widely, you will want to make sure that it supports all attributes of the wrapped resource type. In this case, the `module_file` wrapper should accept all `file` attributes. For example, this is how you add the `mode` attribute to the wrapper type:

```
define module_file(
  String $module,
  Optional[String] $mode = undef
) {
  if $mode != undef {
    File { mode => $mode }
  }
  file { $title:
    source => "puppet:///modules/${module}/${title}"
  }
}
```

The `File { ... }` block declares some default values for all `file` resource attributes in the same scope. The `undef` value is similar to Ruby's `nil`, and is a convenient parameter default value, because it is very unlikely that a user will need to pass it as an actual value for the wrapped resource.

You can employ the override syntax instead of the default syntax as well:

```
File[$name] { mode => $mode }
```

This makes the intent of the code slightly more obvious, but is not necessary in the presence of just one `file` resource. Chapter 6, *The Puppet Beginners Advanced Parts*, holds more information about overrides and defaults.

Using defined types as resource multiplexers

Wrapping single resources with a defined type is useful, but sometimes you will want to add functionality beyond the resource type you are wrapping. At other times, you might wish for your defined type to unify a lot of functionality, just as the comprehensive classes from the beginning of the section.

For both scenarios, what you want to have is multiple resources in the body of your defined type. There is a classic example for this as well:

```
define user_with_key(
   String $key,
   Optional[String] $uid = undef,
   String $group = 'users'
) {
   user { $title:
      ensure      => present
      gid         => $group,
      uid         => $uid,
      managehome => true,
   }
   ssh_authorized_key { "key for ${title}":
      ensure => present,
      user   => $title,
      type   => 'rsa',
      key    => $key,
   }
}
```

This code allows you to create user accounts with authorized SSH keys in one resource declaration. This code sample has some notable aspects:

- Since you are essentially wrapping multiple resource types, the titles of all inner resources are derived from the instance title (or name) of the current defined type instance; actually, this is a required practice for all defined types
- You can hardcode parts of your business logic; in this example, we dispensed with the support for non-RSA SSH keys and defined users as the default group

Using defined types as macros

Some source code requires many repetitive tasks. Assume that your site uses a subsystem that relies on symbolic links at a certain location to enable configuration files, just as init does with the symlinks in rc2.d/ and its siblings, which point back to ../init.d/<service>.

A manifest that enables a large number of configuration snippets might look the same as this:

```
file { '/etc/example_app/conf.d.enabled/england':
  ensure => 'link',
  target => '../conf.d.available/england'
}
file { '/etc/example_app/conf.d.enabled/ireland':
  ensure => 'link',
  target => '../conf.d.available/ireland'
}
file { '/etc/example_app/conf.d.enabled/germany':
  ensure => 'link',
  target => '../conf.d.available/germany'
  ...
}
```

This is tiring to read and somewhat painful to maintain. In a C program, one would use a preprocessor macro that just takes the base name of both link and target and expands to the three lines of each resource description. Puppet does not use a preprocessor, but you can use defined types to achieve a similar result:

```
define example_app_config {
  file { "/etc/example_app/conf.d.enabled/${title}":
    ensure => 'link',
    target => "../conf.d.available/${title}",
  }
}
```

 The defined type actually acts more as a simple function call than an actual macro.

The define requires no arguments, it can rely solely on its resource name, so the preceding code can now be simplified to the following:

```
example_app_config {'england': }
example_app_config {'ireland': }
example_app_config {'germany': }
  ...
```

Alternatively, the following code is even more terse:

```
example_app_config { [ 'england', 'ireland', 'germany', ... ]:
}
```

This array notation leads us to another use of defined types.

Exploiting array values using defined types

One of the more common scenarios in programming is the requirement to accept an array value from some source and perform a task on each value. Puppet manifests are not exempt from this.

Let's assume that the symbolic links from the previous example actually led to directories, and that each such directory would contain a subdirectory to hold optional links to regions. Puppet should manage those links as well.

Of course, after learning about the macro aspect of defined types, you would not want to add each of those regions as distinct resources to your manifest. However, you will need to devise a way to map region names to countries. Seeing as there is already a defined resource type for countries, there is a very direct approach to this: make the list of regions an attribute (or rather, a parameter) of the defined type:

```
define example_app_config (
  Array $regions = []
) {
  file { "/etc/example_app/conf.d.enabled/${name}":
    ensure => link,
    target => "../conf.d.available/${name}",
  }
  # to do: add functionality for $regions
}
```

Using the parameter is straightforward:

```
example_app_config { 'england':
  regions => [ 'South East', 'London' ],
}
example_app_config { 'ireland':
  regions => [ 'Connacht', 'Ulster' ],
}
example_app_config { 'germany':
  regions => [ 'Berlin', 'Bayern', 'Hamburg' ],
}
...
```

The actual challenge is putting these values to use. A naïve approach is to add the following to the definition of `example_app_config`:

```
file { $regions:
    path    => "/etc/example_app/conf.d.enabled/${title}/
      regions/${name}",
    ensure => 'link',
    target => "../../regions.available/${name}";
}
```

However, this will not work. The `$name` variable does not refer to the title of the `file` resource that is being declared. It actually refers, just like `$title`, to the name of the enclosing class or defined type (in this case, the country name). Still, the actual construct will seem quite familiar to you. The only missing piece here is yet another defined type:

```
define example_app_region(String $country) {
    file { "/etc/example_app/conf.d.enabled/${country}/regions/${title}":
        ensure => 'link',
        target => "../../regions.available/${title}",
    }
}
```

The complete definition of the `example_app_config` defined type should look like this then:

```
define example_app_config(Array $regions = []) {
    file { "/etc/example_app/conf.d.enabled/${title}":
        ensure => 'link',
        target => "../conf.d.available/${title}",
    }
    example_app_region { $regions:
      country => $title,
    }
}
```

The *outer* defined type adapts the behavior of the `example_app_region` type to its respective needs by passing its own resource name as a parameter value.

Using iterator functions

With Puppet 4 and later versions, you probably would not write code like the one in the previous section. Thanks to new language features, using defined types as iterators is no longer necessary. We will outline the alternative using the following examples, with a more thorough exploration in Chapter 7, *New Features from Puppet 4 and 5*.

The plain country links can now be declared from an Array using the `each` function:

```
[ 'england', 'ireland', 'germany' ].each |$country| {
  file { "/etc/example_app/conf.d.enabled/${country}":
    ensure => 'link',
    target => "../conf.d.available/${country}",
  }
}
```

The regions can be declared from structured data. A hash suffices for this use case:

```
$region_data = {
  'england' => [ 'South East', 'London' ],
  'ireland' => [ 'Connacht', 'Ulster' ],
  'germany' => [ 'Berlin', 'Bayern', 'Hamburg' ],
}
$region_data.each |$country, $region_array| {
  $region_array.each |$region| {
    file { "/etc/example_app/conf.d.enabled/${country}/
    regions/${region}":
    ensure => link,
    target => "../../regions.available/${region}",
    }
  }
}
```

In new manifests, you should opt for iteration using the `each` and `map` functions over using defined types for this purpose. You will find examples of the former in older manifest code, however. See `Chapter 7`, *New Features from Puppet 4 and 5*, for more information on the topic.

Including classes from defined types

The `example_app_config` type that was defined in the previous example is supposed to serve a very specific purpose. Therefore, it assumes that the base directory, `/etc/example_app`, and its subdirectories were managed independently, outside the defined type. This was a sound design, but many defined types are meant to be used from lots of independent classes or other defined types. Such defines need to be self-contained.

In our example, the defined type needs to make sure that the following resources are part of the manifest:

```
file { [ '/etc/example_app', '/etc/example_app/config.d.enabled' ]:
  ensure => 'directory',
}
```

Just putting this declaration into the body of the define will lead to duplicate resource errors. Each instance of `example_app_config` will try to declare the directories by itself. However, we already have discussed a pattern to avoid just that issue we called it the component class.

To make sure that any instance of the `example_app_config` type is self-contained and works on its own, wrap the preceding declaration in a class (for example, `class example_app_config_directories`) and make sure you include this class right in the body of the define:

```
define example_app_config(Array $regions = []) {
  include example_app_config_directories
  ...
}
```

> You can refer to the examples that come with your copy of this book for the definition of the class.

Ordering and events among classes

Puppet's classes bear little or no similarity to classes that you find in object-oriented programming languages such as Java or Ruby. There are no methods or attributes. There are no distinct instances of any class. You cannot create interfaces or abstract base classes.

One of the few shared characteristics is the encapsulation aspect. Just like classes from OOP, Puppet's classes hide implementation details. To get Puppet to start managing a subsystem, you just need to include the appropriate class.

Passing events between classes and defined types

By sorting all resources into classes, you make it unnecessary (for your co-workers or other collaborators) to know about each single resource. This is beneficial. You can think of the collection of classes and defined types as your interface. You would not want to read all of the manifests that anyone on your project ever wrote.

However, the encapsulation is inconvenient for passing resource events. Say you have a daemon that creates live statistics from your Apache log files. It should subscribe to Apache's configuration files so that it can restart if there are any changes (which might be of consequence to this daemon's operation). In another scenario, you might have Puppet manage some external data for a self-compiled Apache module. If Puppet updates such data, you will want to trigger a restart of the Apache service to reload everything.

Armed with the knowledge that there is a service, `Service['apache2']`, defined somewhere in the `apache` class, you can just go ahead and have your module data files notify that resource. It would work Puppet does not apply any sort of protection to resources that are declared in foreign classes. However, it would pose a minor maintainability issue.

The reference to the resource is located far from the resource itself. When maintaining the manifest later, you or a coworker might wish to look at the resource when encountering the reference. In the case of Apache, it's not difficult to figure out where to look, but in other scenarios, the location of the reference target can be less obvious.

Looking up a targeted resource is usually not necessary, but it can be important to find out what that resource actually does. It gets especially important during debugging, if after a change to the manifest, the referenced resource is no longer found.

Besides, this approach will not work for the other scenario, in which your daemon needs to subscribe to configuration changes. You could blindly subscribe the central `apache2.conf` file, of course. However, this would not yield the desired results if the responsible class opted to do most of the configuration work inside snippets in `/etc/apache2/conf.d`.

Both scenarios can be addressed cleanly and elegantly by directing the `notify` or `subscribe` parameters at the whole class that is managing the entity in question:

```
file { '/var/lib/apache2/sample-module/data01.bin':
  source => '...',
  notify => Class['apache'],
}
service { 'apache-logwatch':
  enable    => true,
  subscribe => Class['apache'],
}
```

Of course, the signals are now sent (or received) indiscriminately the file not only notifies `Service['apache2']`, but also every other resource in the `apache` class. This is usually acceptable, because most resources ignore events.

As for the `logwatch` daemon, it might refresh itself needlessly if a resource in the `apache` class needs a sync action. The odds for this occurrence depend on the implementation of the class. For ideal results, it might be sensible to relocate the configuration file resources into their own class so that the daemon can subscribe to that instead.

With your defined types, you can apply the same rules: subscribe to and notify them as required. Doing so feels quite natural, because they are declared like native resources anyway. This is how you subscribe several instances of the defined type, `symlink`:

```
$active_countries = [ 'England', 'Ireland', 'Germany' ]
service { 'example-app':
  enable     => true,
  subscribe => Symlink[$active_countries],
}
```

Granted, this very example is a bit awkward, because it requires all `symlink` resource titles to be available in an array variable. In this case, it would be more natural to make the defined type instances notify the service instead:

```
symlink { [ 'England', 'Ireland', 'Germany' ]:
  notify => Service['example-app'],
}
```

This notation passes a metaparameter to a defined type. The result is that this parameter value is applied to all resources declared inside the define.

If a defined type wraps or contains a `service` or `exec` type resource, it can also be desirable to notify an instance of that define to refresh the contained resource. The following example assumes that the `service` type is wrapped by a defined type called `protected_service`:

```
file { '/etc/example_app/main.conf':
  source => '...',
  notify => Protected_service['example-app'],
}
```

Ordering containers

The `notify` and `subscribe` metaparameters are not the only ones that you can direct at classes and instances of defined types the same holds `true` for their siblings, `before` and `require`. These allow you to define an order for your resources relative to classes, order instances of your defined types, and even order classes among themselves.

The latter works by virtue of the chaining operator:

```
include firewall
include loadbalancing
Class['firewall'] -> Class['loadbalancing']
```

The effect of this code is that all resources from the `firewall` class will be synchronized before any resource from the `loadbalancing` class, and failure of any resource in the former class will prevent all resources in the latter from being synchronized.

 The chaining arrow cannot just be placed in between the `include` statements. It works only between resource definitions or resource references.

Because of these ordering semantics, it is actually quite wholesome to require a whole class. You effectively mark the resource in question as being dependent on the class. As a result, it will only be synchronized if the entire subsystem that the class models is successfully synchronized first.

Limitations

Sadly, there is a rather substantial issue with both the ordering of containers and the distribution of refresh events: neither will transcend the `include` statements of further classes. Consider the following example:

```
class apache {
  include apache::service
  include apache::package
  include apache::config
}
file { '/etc/apache2/conf.d/passwords.conf':
  source  => '...',
  require => Class['apache'],
}
```

I have often mentioned how the comprehensive `apache` class models everything about the Apache server subsystem, and in the previous section, I went on to explain that directing a `require` parameter at such a class will make sure that Puppet only touches the dependent resource if the subsystem has been successfully configured.

This is mostly true, but, due to the limitation concerning class boundaries, it doesn't achieve the desired effect in this scenario. The dependent configuration file should actually require the `Package['apache']` package, declared in `class apache::package`. However, the relationship does not span multiple class inclusions, so this particular dependency will not be part of the resulting catalog at all.

Similarly, any refresh events sent to the `apache` class will have no effect; they are distributed to resources declared in the class's body (of which there are none), but are not passed on to included classes. Subscribing to the class will make no sense either, because any resource events generated inside the included classes will not be forwarded by the `apache` class.

The bottom line is that relationships to classes cannot be built in utter ignorance of their implementation. If in doubt, you need to make sure that the resources that are of interest are actually declared directly inside the class you are targeting.

 The discussion revolved around the example of the `include` statements in classes, but since it is common to use them in defined types as well; the same limitation applies in this case too.

There is a bright side to this as well. A more correct implementation of the Apache configuration file from the example explained would depend on the package, but would also synchronize itself before the service, and perhaps even notify it (so that Apache restarts if necessary). When all resources are part of the `apache` class and you want to adhere to the pattern of interacting with the container only, it would lead to the following declaration:

```
file { '/etc/apache2/conf.d/passwords.conf':
  source  => '...',
  require => Class['apache'],
  notify  => Class['apache'],
}
```

This forms an instant dependency circle: the `file` resource requires all parts of the `apache` class to be synchronized before it gets processed, but to notify them, they must all be put after the `file` resource in the order graph. This cannot work. With the knowledge of the inner structure of the `apache` class, the user can pick metaparameter values that actually work:

```
file { '/etc/apache2/conf.d/passwords.conf':
  source  => '...',
  require => Class['apache::package'],
  notify  => Class['apache::service'],
}
```

For the curious, the preceding code shows what the inner classes look like, roughly.

The other good news is that invoking defined types does not pose the same kind of issue that an `include` statement of a class does. Events are passed to resources inside defined types just fine, transcending an arbitrary number of stacked invocations. Ordering also works just as expected. Let's keep the example brief:

```
class apache {
  virtual_host { 'example.net': ... }
  ...
}
```

This `apache` class also creates a virtual host using the defined type, `virtual_host`. A resource that requires this class will implicitly require all resources from within this `virtual_host` instance. A subscriber to the class will receive events from those resources, and events directed at the class will reach the resources of this `virtual_host`.

There is actually a good reason to make the `include` statements behave differently in this regard. As classes can be included very generously (thanks to their singleton aspect), it is common for classes to build a vast network of includes. By adding a single `include` statement to a manifest, you might unknowingly pull hundreds of classes into this manifest. Assume, for a moment, that relationships and events transcend this whole network. All manner of unintended effects would be the consequence. Dependency circles would be almost inevitable. The whole construct would become utterly unmanageable. The cost of such relationships would also grow exponentially. Refer to the next section.

The performance implications of container relationships

There is another aspect that you should keep in mind whenever you are referencing a container type to build a relationship to it. The Puppet agent will have to build a dependency graph from this. This graph contains all resources as nodes and all relationships as edges. Classes and defined types get expanded to all their declared resources. All relationships to the container are expanded to relationships to each resource.

This is mostly harmless if the other end of the relationship is a native resource. A file that requires a class with five declared resources leads to five dependencies. That does not hurt. It gets more interesting if the same class is required by an instance of a defined type that comprises three resources. Each of these builds a relationship to each of the class's resources, so you end up with 15 edges in the graph.

It gets even more expensive when a container invokes complex defined types, perhaps even recursively.

A more complex graph means more work for the Puppet agent, and its runs will take longer. This is especially annoying when running agents interactively during the debugging or development of your manifest. To avoid the unnecessary effort, consider your relationship declarations carefully, and use them only when they are really appropriate.

Mitigating the limitations

The architects of the Puppet language have devised two alternative approaches to solve the ordering issues. We will consider both, because you might encounter them in existing manifests. In new setups, you should always choose the latter variant.

The anchor pattern

The `anchor` pattern is the classic workaround for the problem with ordering and signaling in the context of recursive class `include` statements. It can be illustrated by the following example class:

```
class example_app {
  anchor { 'example_app::begin':
    notify => Class['example_app_config'],
  }
  include example_app_config
  anchor { 'example_app::end':
```

```
    require => Class['example_app_config'],
  }
}
```

Consider a resource that is placed `before=> Class['example_app']`. It ends up in the chain before each `anchor`, and therefore, also before any resource in `example_app_config`, despite the `include` limitation. This is because the `Anchor['example_app::begin']` pseudo-resource notifies the included class and is therefore ordered before all of its resources. A similar effect works for objects that require the class, by virtue of the `example::end` anchor.

The `anchor` resource type was created for this express purpose. It is not part of the Puppet core, but has been made available through the `stdlib` module instead (the next chapter will familiarize you with modules). Since it also forwards refresh events, it is even possible to notify and subscribe this anchored class, and events will propagate into and out of the included `example_app_config` class.

The `stdlib` module is available in the Puppet Forge, but more about this in the next chapter. There is a descriptive document for the `anchor` pattern to be found online as well, in Puppet documentation at `http://projects.puppetlabs.com/projects/puppet/wiki/Anchor_Pattern`. It is somewhat dated, given that the anchor pattern has been supplanted as well by Puppet's ability to contain a class in a container.

The contain function

To make composite classes work directly around the limitations of the `include` statement, you can take advantage of the `contain` function found in Puppet version 3.4.x or newer.

If the earlier `apache` example had been written like the following one, there would have been no issues concerning ordering and refresh events:

```
class apache {
  contain apache::service
  contain apache::package
  contain apache::config
}
```

The official documentation describes the behavior as follows:

> *"A contained class will not be applied before the containing class is begun, and will be finished before the containing class is finished."*

This might read like we're now discussing the panacea for the presented class ordering issues here. Should you just be using `contain` in place of `include` from here on out and never worry about class ordering again? Of course not; this would introduce lots of unnecessary ordering constraints and lead you into unfixable dependency circles very quickly. Do contain classes, but make sure that it makes sense. The contained class should really form a vital part of what the containing class is modeling.

The quoted documentation refers to classes only, but classes can be contained in defined types just as well. The effect of containment is not limited to ordering aspects either. Refresh events are also correctly propagated.

Making classes more flexible through parameters

Up until this point, classes and defines were presented as direct opposites with respect to flexibility; defined types are inherently adaptable through different parameter values, whereas classes model just one static piece of state. As the section title suggests, this is not entirely true. Classes, too, can have parameters. Their definition and declaration become rather similar to those of defined types in this case:

```
class apache::config(Integer $max_clients=100) {
  file { '/etc/apache2/conf.d/max_clients.conf':
    content => "MaxClients ${max_clients}\n",
  }
}
```

With a definition like the preceding one, the class can be declared with a parameter value:

```
class { 'apache::config':
  max_clients => 120,
}
```

This enables some very elegant designs, but introduces some drawbacks as well.

The caveats of parameterized classes

The consequence of allowing class parameters is almost obvious: you lose the singleton characteristic. Well, that's not entirely true either, but your freedom in declaring the class gets limited drastically.

Classes that define default values for all parameters can still be declared with the `include` statement. This can still be done an arbitrary number of times in the same manifest.

However, the resource like declaration of `class { 'name': }` cannot appear more than once for any given class in the same manifest. This is in keeping with the rules for resources and should not be very surprising-after all, it would be very awkward to try to bind different values to a class's parameters in different locations throughout the manifest.

Things become very confusing when mixing `include` with the alternative syntax though. It is valid to include a class an arbitrary number of times after it has been declared using the resource-like notation. However, you cannot use the resource style declaration after a class has been declared using `include`. That's because the parameters are then determined to assume their default values, and a `class { 'name': }` declaration clashes with that.

In a nutshell, the following code works:

```
class { 'apache::config': }
include apache::config
```

However, the following code does not work:

```
include apache::config
class { 'apache::config': }
```

As a consequence, you effectively cannot add parameters to component classes, because the `include` statement is no longer safe to use in large quantities. Therefore, parameters are essentially only useful for comprehensive classes, which usually don't get included from different parts of the manifest.

In `Chapter 5`, *Combining Classes, Configuration Files, and Extensions into Modules*, we will discuss some alternate patterns, some of which exploit class parameters. Also note that Chapter 8, *Separation of Code and Data with Hiera*, presents a solution that gives you more flexibility with parameterized classes. Using this, you can be more liberal with your class interfaces.

Preferring the include keyword

Ever since class parameters have been available, some Puppet users have felt compelled to write (example) code that would make it a point to forgo the `include` keyword in favor of resource-like class declarations, such as this:

```
class apache {
  class { 'apache::service': }
  class { 'apache::package': }
  class { 'apache::config': }
}
```

Doing this is a very bad idea. We cannot stress this enough: one of the most powerful concepts about Puppet's classes is their singleton aspect the ability to include a class in a manifest arbitrarily and without worrying about clashes with other code. The mentioned declaration syntax deprives you of this power, even when the classes in question don't support parameters.

The safest route is to use `include` whenever possible, and to avoid the alternate syntax whenever you can. In fact, Chapter 8, *Separation of Code and Data with Hiera*, introduces the ability to use class parameters without the resource same as class declaration. This way, you can rely solely on `include`, even when parameters are in play. These are the safest recommended practices to keep you out of trouble from incompatible class declarations.

Summary

Classes and defined types are the essential tools to create reusable Puppet code. While classes hold resources that must not be repeated in a manifest, the define is capable of managing a distinct set of adapted resources upon every invocation. It does that by leveraging the parameter values it receives. While classes do support parameters as well, there are some caveats to bear in mind.

To use defined types in your manifest, you declare instances just like resources of native types. Classes are mainly used through the `include` statement, although there are alternatives such as the `class { }` syntax or the `contain` function. There are also some ordering issues with classes that the `contain` function can help mitigate. In theory, classes and defines suffice to build almost all the manifests that you will ever need. In practice, you will want to organize your code into larger structures.

The `Chapter 5`, *Combining Classes, Configuration Files, and Extensions into Modules*, will show you how to do exactly that, and introduce you to a whole range of useful functionality beyond it.

5
Combining Classes, Configuration Files, and Extensions into Modules

In the previous chapter, you learned about the tools that create modularized and reusable Puppet code in the form of classes and defined types. We discussed that almost all Puppet resources should be separated into appropriate classes, except if they logically need to be part of a defined type. This is almost enough syntax to build manifests for an entire fleet of agent nodes; each selecting the appropriate composite classes, which in turn include further required classes, with all the classes recursively instantiating the defined types.

What has not been discussed up until now is the organization of the manifests in the filesystem. It is obviously undesirable to stuff all of your code into one large `site.pp` file. The answer to this problem is provided by modules and will be explained in this chapter.

Besides organizing classes and defines, modules are also a way to share common code. They are software libraries for Puppet manifests and plugins. They also offer a convenient place to locate the interface descriptions that were hinted at in the previous chapter. Puppet Labs runs a dedicated service for hosting open source modules, called the Puppet Forge.

The existence and general location of the modules were mentioned briefly in Chapter 3, *A Peek into the Ruby Part of Puppet - Facts, Types, and Providers*. It is now time to explore these and other aspects in greater detail. We'll cover the following topics in this chapter:

- The contents of Puppet's modules
- Managing environments
- Building a component module
- Finding helpful Forge modules

The contents of Puppet's modules

A module can be seen as a higher-order organizational unit. It bundles up classes and defined types that contribute to a common management goal (specific system aspects or a piece of software, for example). These manifests are not all that is organized through modules; most modules also bundle files and file templates. There can also be several kinds of Puppet plugins in a module. This section will explain these different parts of a module and show you where they are located. You will also learn about the means of module documentation and how to obtain existing modules for your own use.

Parts of a module

For most modules, **manifests** form the most important part - the core functionality. The manifests consist of classes and defined types, which all share a namespace, rooted at the module name. For example, an `ntp` module will contain only classes and defines whose names start with the `ntp::` prefix.

Many modules contain files that can be synced to the agent's filesystem. This is often used for configuration files or snippets. You have seen examples of this, but let's repeat them. A frequent occurrence in many manifests is `file` resources such as the following:

```
file { '/etc/ntp.conf':
  source => 'puppet:///modules/ntp/ntp.conf',
}
```

The previous resource references a file that ships with a hypothetical `ntp` module. It has been prepared to provide generally suitable configuration data. However, there is often the need to tweak some parameters inside such a file, so that the node manifests can declare customized config settings for the respective agent. The tool of choice for this is templates, which will be discussed in `Chapter 6`, *The Puppet Beginners Advanced Parts*.

Another possible component of a module that you have already read about is custom facts-code that gets synchronized to the agent and runs before a catalog is requested, so that the output becomes available as facts about the agent system.

These facts are not the only Puppet plugins that can be shipped with modules. There are also **parser functions** (also called **custom functions**), for one. These are actual functions that you can use in your manifests. In many situations, they are the most convenient way, if not the only way, to build some specific implementations.

The final plugin type that has also been hinted at in an earlier chapter is the custom native types and providers, which are conveniently placed in modules as well.

Module structure

All the mentioned components need to be located in specific filesystem locations for the master to pick them up. Each module forms a directory tree. Its root is named after the module itself. For example, the `ntp` module is stored in a directory called `ntp/`.

All manifests are stored in a subdirectory called `manifests/`. Each class and defined type has its own respective file. The `ntp::package` class will be found in `manifests/package.pp`, and the defined type called `ntp::monitoring::nagios` will be found in `manifests/monitoring/nagios.pp`. The first particle of the container name (`ntp`) is always the module name, and the rest describes the location under `manifests/`. You can refer to the module tree in the following paragraphs for more examples.

The `manifests/init.pp` file is special. It can be thought of as a default manifest location, because it is looked up for any definition from the module in question.

Both the examples that were just mentioned can be put into `init.pp` and will still work. Doing this makes it harder to locate the definitions, though.

In practice, `init.pp` should only hold one class, which is named after the module (such as the `ntp` class), if your module implements such a class. This is a common practice, as it allows the manifests to use a simple statement to tap the core functionality of the module:

```
include ntp
```

You can refer to the *Module best practices* section for some more notes on this subject.

The files and templates that a module serves to the agents are not this strictly sorted into specific locations. It is only important that they be placed in the `files/` and `templates/` subdirectories, respectively. The contents of these subtrees can be structured to the module author's liking, and the manifest must reference them correctly. Static files should always be addressed through URLs, such as these:

```
puppet:///modules/ntp/ntp.conf
puppet:///modules/my_app/opt/scripts/find_my_app.sh
```

These files are found in the corresponding subdirectories of `files/`:

```
.../modules/ntp/files/ntp.conf
.../modules/my_app/files/opt/scripts/find_my_app.sh
```

The `modules` prefix in the URI is mandatory and is always followed by the module name. The rest of the path translates directly to the contents of the `files/` directory. There are similar rules for templates. You can refer to `Chapter 6`, *The Puppet Beginners Advanced Parts*, for the details.

Finally, all plugins are located in the `lib/` subtree. Custom facts are Ruby files in `lib/facter/`. Parser functions are stored in `lib/puppet/parser/functions/`, the Puppet 4 API functions are located in `lib/puppet/functions/`, and for custom resource types and providers, there is `lib/puppet/type/` and `lib/puppet/provider/`, respectively. This is not a coincidence; these Ruby libraries are looked up by the master and the agent in the according namespaces. There are examples for all these components later in this chapter.

In short, the following are the contents of a possible module in a tree view:

```
/opt/puppetlabs/code/environments/production/modules/my_app
    |- templates/ # templates are covered in the next chapter
    |- files/
    | |- subdir1/ # puppet:///modules/my_app/subdir1/<filename>
    | |- subdir2/ # puppet:///modules/my_app/subdir2/<filename>
    | | \- subsubdir/ # puppet:///modules/my_app/subdir2/subsubdir/...
    |- manifests/
    | |- init.pp # class my_app is defined here
```

```
|  |- params.pp # class my_app::params is defined here
|  |- config/
|  |  |- detail.pp # my_app::config::detail is defined here
|  |  \- basics.pp # my_app::config::basics is defined here
\- lib/
      |- facter/ # contains .rb files with custom facts
      \- puppet/
          |- functions # contains .rb files with Puppet 4 functions
          |- parser/
          |  \- functions # contains .rb files with parser functions
          |- type/ # contains .rb files with custom types
          \- provider/ # contains .rb files with custom providers
```

Documentation in modules

A module can and should include documentation. The Puppet master does not process any module documentation by itself. As such, it is largely up to the authors to decide how to structure the documentation of the modules that are created for their specific site only. That being said, there are some common practices, and it's a good idea to adhere to them. Besides, if a module should end up being published on the Forge, appropriate documentation should be considered mandatory.

 The process of publishing modules is beyond the scope of this book. You can find a guide at `https://docs.puppetlabs.com/puppet/latest/ reference/modules_publishing.html`.

For many modules, the main focus of the documentation is centered on the README file, which is located right in the module's root directory. It is customarily formatted in Markdown as README.md or README.markdown. The README file should contain explanations and, often, there is a reference documentation as well.

Puppet DSL interfaces can also be documented right in the manifest, in the rdoc and YARD format. This applies to classes and defined types:

```
# Class: my_app::firewall
#
# @summary This class adds firewall rules to allow access to my_app.
#
# @example Declaring the class
# include my_app::firewall
#
# @param Parameters: none
class my_app::firewall {
```

```
    # class code here
}
```

You can generate HTML documentation (including navigation) for all your modules using the `puppet strings` subcommand. This subcommand is available after installation of the puppet-strings Ruby extension: `puppet resource package puppet-strings provider=puppet_gem`. This practice is somewhat obscure, so it won't be discussed here in great detail. However, if this option is attractive to you, we encourage you to peruse the documentation.

The following command provides an overview of possible puppet strings functionality:

```
puppet help strings
```

Managing environments

Puppet doesn't organize things in modules exclusively. There is a higher-level unit called **environment** that groups and contains the modules. An environment mainly consists of:

- One or more site manifest files
- A `modules` directory with your modules inside
- An optional `environment.conf` configuration file

When the master compiles the manifest for a node, it uses exactly one environment for this task. As described in Chapter 2, *Puppet Server and Agents*, it always starts in `manifests/*.pp`, which form the environment's site manifest. Before we take a look at how this works in practice, let's look at an example `environment` directory:

```
/opt/puppetlabs/code/environments/
    \- production/
        |- environment.conf
        |- manifests/
        | |- site.pp
        | \- nodes.pp
        \- modules/
            |- my_app/
            \- ntp/
```

The `environment.conf` file can customize the environment. Normally, Puppet uses `site.pp` and the other files in the `manifests` directory. To make Puppet read all the `pp` files in another directory, set the `manifest` option in `environment.conf`:

```
#/opt/puppetlabs/code/environments/production/environment.conf
manifest = puppet_manifests
```

In most circumstances, the manifest option need not be changed.

The `site.pp` file will include node classification with classes from the modules. Puppet looks for modules in the `modules` subdirectory of the active environment. You can define additional subdirectories that hold the modules by setting the `modulepath` option in `environment.conf`:

```
#/opt/puppetlabs/code/environments/production/environment.conf
modulepath = modules:site-modules
```

The directory structure can be made more distinctive:

```
/opt/puppetlabs/code/environments/
    \- production/
        |- manifests/
        |- modules/
        | \- ntp/
        \- site-modules/
            \- my_app/
```

Configuring environment locations

Puppet uses the `production` environment by default. This and the other environments are expected to be located in `/opt/puppetlabs/code/environments`. You can override this default by setting the `environmentpath` option in `puppet.conf`:

```
[main]
environmentpath = /etc/local/puppet/environments
```

Obtaining and installing modules

Downloading existing modules is very common. Puppet Labs hosts a dedicated site for sharing and obtaining the modules - the Puppet Forge. It works just the same as RubyGems or CPAN and makes it simple for the user to retrieve a given module through a command-line interface. In the Forge, the modules are fully named by prefixing the actual module name with the author's name, such as `puppetlabs-stdlib` or `ffrank-constraints`.

The `puppet module install` command installs a module in the active environment:

```
root@puppetmaster# puppet module install puppetlabs-stdlib
```

The *Testing your modules* section has information on using different environments.

The current release of the `stdlib` module (authored by the user `puppetlabs`) is downloaded from the Forge and installed in the standard modules' location. This is the first location in the current environment's `modulepath`, which is usually the `modules` subdirectory. Specifically, the modules will most likely end up in the `environments/production/modules` directory.

The `stdlib` module in particular should be considered mandatory; it adds a large number of useful functions to the Puppet language. Examples include the `keys`, `values`, and `has_key` functions, which are essential for implementing the proper handling of hash structures, to name only a few. The functions are available to your manifests as soon as the module is installed, there is no need to include any class or other explicit loading. If you write your own modules that add functions, these are loaded automatically in the same way.

Module best practices

With all the current versions of Puppet, you should make it a habit to put all the manifest code into modules, with only the following few exceptions:

- The `node` blocks
- The `include` statements for very select classes that should be omnipresent (the most common design pattern does this in the so-called base role, however; see Chapter 9, *Puppet Roles and Profiles*, for the roles and profiles pattern)

- Declarations of helpful variables that should have the same availability as the Facter facts in your manifests

This section provides details on how to organize your manifests accordingly. It also advises some design practices and strategies in order to test the changes to the modules.

Putting everything in modules

You might find some manifests in very old installations that gather lots of manifest files in one or more directories and use the `import` statements in the `site.pp` file, such as:

```
import '/etc/puppet/manifests/custom/*.pp'
```

All classes and defined types in these files are then available globally.

This whole approach had scalability issues and has long been deprecated. The `import` keyword is missing from Puppet 4 and the newer versions.

It is far more efficient to give meaningful names to the classes and defined types so that Puppet can look them up in the collection of modules. The scheme has been discussed in an earlier section already, so let's just look at another example where the Puppet compiler encounters a class name, such as:

```
include ntp::server::component::watchdog
```

Puppet will go ahead and locate the `ntp` module in all the configured module locations of the active environment (path names in the `modulepath` setting). It will then try and read the `ntp/manifests/server/component/watchdog.pp` file in order to find the class definition. Failing this, it will try `ntp/manifests/init.pp`.

This makes compilation very efficient. Puppet dynamically identifies the required manifest files and includes only those for parsing. It also aids code inspection and development, as it is abundantly clear where you should look for specific definitions.

Technically, it is possible to stuff all of a module's manifests into its `init.pp` file, but you lose the advantages that a structured tree of module manifests offers.

Avoiding generalization

Each module should ideally serve a specific purpose. On a site that relies on Puppet to manage a diverse server infrastructure, there are likely modules for each respective service, such as apache, ssh, nagios, nginx, and so forth. Most of these modules will be taken from an upstream development and are referred to as "technical component modules". There can also be site-specific modules, such as users or shell_settings, if the operations require this kind of fine-grained control. Such customized modules are sometimes just named after the group or the company that owns them.

The ideal granularity depends on the individual requirements of your setup. What you generally want to avoid are modules with names such as utilities or helpers, which serve as a melting pot for ideas that don't fit in any of the existing modules. Such a lack of organization can be detrimental to discipline and can lead to chaotic modules that include definitions that should have become their own respective modules instead.

Adding more modules is cheap. A module generally incurs no cost for the Puppet master operation, and your user experience will usually become more efficient with more modules, not less so. Of course, this balance can tip if your site imposes special documentation or other handling prerequisites on each module. Such rulings must then be weighed into the decisions about module organization.

Testing your modules

Depending on the size of your agent network, some or many of your modules can be used by a large variety of nodes. Despite these commonalities, these nodes can be quite different from one another. A change to a central module, such as ssh or ntp, which are likely used by a large number of agents, can have quite extensive consequences.

The first and the most important tool for testing your work is the --noop option for Puppet. It works for puppet agent, as well as puppet apply. If it is given on the command-line, Puppet will not perform any necessary sync actions, and will merely present the respective line of output to you instead. There is an example of this in Chapter 1, *Writing Your First Manifests*.

When using a master instead of working locally with puppet apply, a new problem arises, though. The master is queried by all your agents. Unless all the agents are disabled while you are testing a new manifest, it is very likely that one will check in and accidentally run the untested code.

In fact, even your test agent can trigger its regular run while you are logged in, transparently in the background.

It is very important to guard against such uncontrolled manifest applications. A small mistake can damage a number of agent machines in a short time period. The best way to go about this is to define multiple environments on the master and stage code changes. `Chapter 9`, *Puppet Roles and Profiles*, will provide further information on this topic.

Safe testing with environments

Besides the `production` environment, you should create at least one testing environment. You can call it `testing` or whatever you like. When using the directory environments, just create its directory in `environmentpath`.

Such an additional environment is very useful for testing changes. The test environment or environments should be copies of the production data. Prepare all the manifest changes in `testing` first. You can make your agents test this change before you copy it to production:

```
root@agent# puppet agent --test --noop --environment testing
```

You can even omit the `noop` flag on some or all of your agents so that the change is actually deployed. Some subtle mistakes in the manifests cannot be detected from an inspection of the `noop` output, so it is usually a good idea to run the code at least once before releasing it.

Environments are even more effective when used in conjunction with source control, especially distributed systems such as `git` or `mercurial`. Versioning your Puppet code is a good idea independently of environments and testing; this is one of the greatest advantages that Puppet has to offer you through its infrastructure as code paradigm.

Using environments and the `noop` mode form a pragmatic approach to testing that can serve in most scenarios. The safety against erroneous Puppet behavior is limited, of course. There are more formal ways of testing the modules:

- The `rspec-puppet` tool allows the module authors to implement unit tests based on `rspec`. You can find more details at `http://rspec-puppet.com/`
- Acceptance testing can be performed through `beaker`. You can refer to `https://github.com/puppetlabs/beaker/wiki/How-To-Beaker` for details

Explaining these tools in detail is beyond the scope of this book.

Building a component module

This chapter has discussed many theoretical and operational aspects of modules, but you are yet to gain an insight into the process of writing modules. For this purpose, the rest of this chapter will have you create an example module step by step.

It should be stressed again that, for the most part, you will want to find general purpose modules from the Forge. The number of available modules is ever-growing, so the odds are good that there is something already there to help you with what you need to do.

Assume that you want to add Cacti to your network: an RRD tool-based trend monitor and graphing server, including a web interface. If you would check the Forge first, you would indeed find some modules. However, let's further assume that none of them speak to you, because either the feature set or the implementation is not to your liking. If even the respective interfaces don't meet your requirements, it doesn't make much sense to base your own module on an existing one (in the form of a fork on GitHub) either. You will, then, need to write your own module from scratch.

Naming your module

Module names should be concise and to the point. If you manage a specific piece of software, name your module after it - `apache`, `java`, `mysql`, and so forth. Avoid verbs such as `install_cacti` or `manage_cacti`. If your module name does need to consist of several words (because the target subsystem has a long name), they should be divided by underscore characters. Spaces, dashes, and other non-alphanumeric characters are not allowed.

In our example, the module should just be named `cacti`.

Usually, you will never write a module with names such as apache, mysql, java, as these are names already used from upstream development. When learning Puppet, one wants to start with a simple module implementation, maybe the upstream module is yet too complicated to understand. In this case, you want to prefix your modules with a company or team name. Keep in mind to not use the hyphen but an underscore to separate company/team name, for example, `packt_apache`, `infra_mysql`. This pattern will keep the original namepsace available and allow easier migration to upstream modules later.

Making your module available to Puppet

To use your own module, you don't need to make it available for installation through `puppet module`. For that, you will need to upload the module to the Forge first, which will require quite some additional effort. Luckily, a module will work just fine without all this preparation, if you just put the source code in the proper location on your master.

To create your own `cacti` module, create the basic directories:

```
root@puppetmaster# mkdir -p
/opt/puppetlabs/code/environments/testing/packt_cacti/{manifests,files}
```

Don't forget to synchronize all the changes to `production` once the agents use them.

Implementing basic module functionality

Most modules perform all of their work through their manifests.

There are notable exceptions, such as the `stdlib` module. It mainly adds the parser functions and a few general-purpose resource types.

When planning the classes for your module, it is most straightforward to think about how you would like to use the finished module. There is a wide range of possible interface designs. The de facto standard stipulates that the managed subsystem is initialized on the agent system by including the module's main class; the class that bears the same name as the module and is implemented in the module's `init.pp` file.

For our Cacti module, the user should use the following:

```
include packt_cacti
```

As a result, Puppet would take all the required steps in order to install the software and, if necessary, perform any additional initialization.

Start by creating the cacti class and implementing the setup in the way you would from the command-line, replacing the commands with appropriate Puppet resources. On a Debian system, installing the cacti package is enough. Other required software is brought in through the dependencies (completing the LAMP stack), and after the package installation, the interface becomes available through the web URI /cacti/ on the server machine:

```
# .../modules/packt_cacti/manifests/init.pp
class packt_cacti {
  package { 'cacti':
    ensure => installed,
  }
}
```

Your module is now ready for testing. Invoke it from your agent's manifest in site.pp or nodes.pp of the testing environment:

```
node 'agent' {
  include packt_cacti
}
```

Apply it on your agent directly:

```
root@agent# puppet agent --test --environment testing
```

This will work on Debian, and Cacti is reachable via http://<address>/cacti/.

 Some sites use an **External Node Classifier** (**ENC**), such as the Foreman. Among other helpful things, it can centrally assign environments to the nodes. In this scenario, the --environment switch will not work.

It's unfortunate that the Cacti web interface will not come up when the home page is requested through the / URI. To enable this, give the module the ability to configure an appropriate redirection. Prepare an Apache configuration snippet in the module in /opt/puppetlabs/code/environments/testing/packt_cacti/files/etc/apache2 /conf.d/cacti-redirect.conf:

```
# Do not edit this file - it is managed by Puppet!
RedirectMatch permanent ^/$ /cacti/
```

The warning notice is helpful, especially when multiple administrators have access to the Cacti server.

It makes sense to add a dedicated class that will sync this file to the agent machine:

```
# .../modules/packt_cacti/manifests/redirect.pp
class packt_cacti::redirect {
  file { '/etc/apache2/conf.d/cacti-redirect.conf':
    ensure => file,
    source => 'puppet:///modules/packt_cacti/etc/apache2/conf.d/cacti-
redirect.conf',
    require => Package['cacti'];
  }
}
```

A short file such as this can also be managed through the file type's content property instead of source:

```
$puppet_warning = '# Do not edit - managed by Puppet!'
$line = 'RedirectMatch permanent ^/$ /cacti/'
file { '/etc/apache2/conf.d/cacti-redirect.conf':
  ensure  => file,
  content => "${puppet_warning}\n${line}\n",
}
```

This is more efficient, because the content is part of the catalog and so the agent does not need to retrieve the checksum through another request to the master.

The module now allows the user to `include packt_cacti::redirect` in order to get this functionality. This is not a bad interface as such, but this kind of modification is actually well-suited to become a parameter of the `cacti` class:

```
class packt_cacti(
  $redirect = true,)
{
  if $redirect {
    contain packt_cacti::redirect
  }
  package { 'cacti':
    ensure => installed,
  }
}
```

The redirect is now installed by default when a manifest uses `include cacti`.
If the web server has other virtual hosts that serve things that are not Cacti, this might be undesirable. In such cases, the manifest will declare the class with the following parameter:

```
class { 'packt_cacti':
  redirect => false,
}
```

Speaking of best practices, most modules will also separate the installation routine into a class of its own. In our case, this is hardly helpful, because the installation status is ensured through a single resource, but let's do it anyway:

```
class packt_cacti(
  $redirect = true,
) {
  contain packt_cacti::install
  if $redirect {
    contain packt_cacti::redirect
  }
}
```

It's sensible to use `contain` here in order to make the Cacti management a solid unit. The `cacti::install` class is put into a separate `install.pp` manifest file:

```
# .../modules/packt_cacti/manifests/install.pp
class packt_cacti::install {
  package { 'cacti':
    ensure => 'installed',
  }
}
```

On Debian, the installation process of the `cacti` package copies another Apache configuration file to `/etc/apache2/conf.d`. Since Puppet performs a normal `apt` installation, this result will be achieved. However, Puppet does not make sure that the configuration stays in this desired state.

 There is an actual risk that the configuration might get broken. If the `puppetlabs-apache` module is in use for a given node, it will usually purge any unmanaged configuration files from the `/etc/apache2/` tree. Be very careful when you enable this module for an existing server. Test it in the `noop` mode. If required, amend the manifest to include the existing configuration.

It is prudent to add a `file` resource to the manifest that keeps the configuration snippet in its post-installation state. Usually with Puppet, this will require you to copy the config file contents to the module, just as the redirect configuration is in a file on the master. However, since the Debian package for Cacti includes a copy of the snippet in `/usr/share/doc/cacti/cacti.apache.conf`, you can instruct the agent to sync the actual configuration with that. Perform this in yet another de facto standard for modules the `config` class:

```
# .../modules/packt_cacti/manifests/config.pp
class packt_cacti::config {
  file { '/etc/apache2/conf.d/cacti.conf':
    mode   => '0644',
    source => '/usr/share/doc/cacti/cacti.apache.conf',
  }
}
```

This class should be contained by the `packt_cacti` class as well. Running the agent again will now have no effect, because the configuration is already in place.

Creating utilities for derived manifests

You have now created several classes that compartmentalize the basic installation and configuration work for your module. Classes lend themselves very well to implementing global settings that are relevant for the managed software as a whole.

However, just installing Cacti and making its web interface available is not an especially powerful capability after all, the module does little beyond what a user can achieve by installing Cacti through the package manager. The much greater pain point with Cacti is that it usually requires configuration via its web interface; adding servers as well as choosing and configuring graphs for each server can be an arduous task and require dozens of clicks per server, depending on the complexity of your graphing needs.

This is where Puppet can be the most helpful. A textual representation of the desired states allows for quick copy and paste repetition and name substitution through regular expressions. Better yet, once there is a Puppet interface, users can devise their own defined types in order to save themselves from the copy and paste work.

Speaking of defined types, they are what is required for your module to allow this kind of configuration. Each machine in Cacti's configuration should be an instance of a defined type. The graphs can have their own type as well.

As with the implementation of the classes, the first thing you always need to ask yourself is how this task would be done from the command-line.

Actually, the better question can be what API you should use for this, preferably from Ruby. However, this is only important if you intend to write Puppet plugins: resource types and providers. We will look into this later in this very chapter.

Cacti comes with a set of CLI scripts. The Debian package makes these available in `/usr/share/cacti/cli`. Let's discover these while we step through the implementation of the Puppet interface. The goals are defined types that will effectively wrap the command-line tools so that Puppet can always maintain the defined configuration state through appropriate queries and update commands.

Adding configuration items

When designing more capabilities for the Cacti module, first comes the ability to register a machine for monitoring - or rather, a **device**, as Cacti itself calls it (network infrastructure such as switches and routers are frequently monitored as well, and not only computers). The name for the first defined type should, therefore, be `cacti::device`.

The same warnings from the *Naming your module* subsection apply - don't give in to the temptation to give names such as `create_device` or `define_domain` to your type, unless you have very good reasons, such as the removal being impossible. Even then, it's probably better to skip the verb.

The CLI script used to register a device is named `add_device.php`. Its help output readily indicate that it requires two parameters, which are `description` and `ip`. A custom description of an entity is often a good use for the respective Puppet resource's title. The type almost writes itself now:

```
# .../modules/packt_cacti/manifests/device.pp
define packt_cacti::device (
  $ip,
) {
  $cli = '/usr/share/cacti/cli'
  $options = "--description='${title}' --ip='${ip}'"
  exec { "add-cacti-device-${title}":
    command => "${cli}/add_device.php ${options}",
    require => Class['cacti'],
}
```

In practice, it is often unnecessary to use so many variables, but it serves readability with the limited horizontal space of the page.

This `exec` resource gives Puppet the ability to use the CLI to create a new device in the Cacti configuration. Since PHP is among the Cacti package's requirements, it's sufficient to make the `exec` resource `require` the `cacti` class. Note the use of `$title`, not only for the `--description` parameter, but in the resource name for the `exec` resource as well. This ensures that each `packt_cacti::device` instance declares a unique `exec` resource in order to create itself.

The `exec` resource type allows one to run arbitrary commands with root privileges and an empty shell environment. This allows one to flexibly wrap configuration commands in puppet DSL. But the exec resource type has its downside: the `exec` resource type is not, per-se idempotent and bares the risk that everything is done with running commands, which is against Puppet's nature of being a declarative configuration management system. The best option is to see the `exec` resource type as an emergency exit: only use it if one sees no other possibilities to achieve the goals.

Usually, a custom resource type is more suitable, especially when running difficult commands with difficult check options. The custom resource type is explained later in this chapter.

However, this still lacks an important aspect. Written as in the preceding example, this exec resource will make the Puppet agent run the CLI script always, under any circumstances. This is incorrect though - it should only run if the device has not yet been added.

Every exec resource should have one of the creates, onlyif, or unless parameters. It defines a query for Puppet to determine the current sync state. The add_device call must be made unless the device exists already. The query for the existing devices must be made through the add_graphs.php script (counterintuitively). When called with the --list-hosts option, it prints one header line and a table of devices, with the description in the fourth column. The following unless query will find the resource in question:

```
$search = "sed 1d | cut -f4- | grep -q '^${title}\$'"
exec { "add-cacti-device-${title}":
  command => "${cli}/add_device.php ${options}",
  path    => '/bin:/usr/bin',
  unless  => "${cli}/add_graphs.php --list-hosts |
             ${search}",
  require => Class[cacti],
}
```

The path parameter is useful, as it allows for calling the core utilities without the respective full path.

It is a good idea to generally set a standard list of search paths, because some tools will not work with an empty PATH environment variable.

The unless command will return 0 if the exact resource title is found among the list of devices. The final $ sign is escaped so that Puppet includes it in the $search command string literally.

You can now test your new define by adding the following resource to the agent machine's manifest:

```
# in manifests/nodes.pp
node 'agent' {
  include packt_cacti
  packt_cacti::device { 'Puppet test agent (Debian 7)':
    ip => $::ipaddress,
  }
}
```

On the next `puppet agent --test` run, you will be notified that the command for adding the device has been run. Repeat the run and Puppet will determine that everything is now already synchronized with the catalog.

Allowing customization

The `add_device.php` script has a range of optional parameters that allow the user to customize the device. The Puppet module should expose these dials as well. Let's pick one and implement it in the `packt_cacti::device` type. Each Cacti device has a `ping_method` that defaults to `tcp`. With the module, we can even superimpose our own defaults over those of the software:

```
define packt_cacti::device(
  $ip,
  $ping_method='icmp'
){
  $cli = '/usr/share/cacti/cli'
  $base_opt = "--description='${title}' --ip='${ip}'"
  $ping_opt = "--ping_method=${ping_method}"
  $options = "${base_opt} ${ping_opt}"
  $search = "sed 1d | cut -f4- | grep -q '^${title}\$'"
  exec { "add-cacti-device-${title}":
    command => "${cli}/add_device.php ${options}",
    path    => '/bin:/usr/bin',
    unless  => "${cli}/add_graphs.php --list-hosts | ${search}",
    require => Class[cacti],
  }
}
```

The module uses a default of `icmp` instead of `tcp`. The value is always passed to the CLI script, whether it was passed to the `packt_cacti::device` instance or not. The parameter default is used in the latter case.

> If you plan to publish your module, it is more sensible to try and use the same defaults as the managed software whenever possible.

Once you incorporate all the available CLI switches, you will have successfully created a Puppet API in order to add devices to your Cacti configuration, giving the user the benefits of easy reproduction, sharing, implicit documentation, simple versioning, and more.

Removing unwanted configuration items

There is still one remaining wrinkle. It is atypical for Puppet types to be unable to remove the entities that they create. As it stands, this is a technical limitation of the CLI that powers your module, because it does not implement a `remove_device` function yet. Such scripts have been made available on the internet, but are not properly a part of Cacti at the time of writing this.

To give the module more functionality, it would make sense to incorporate additional CLI scripts among the module's files. Put the appropriate file into the right directory under `modules/cacti/files/` and add another `file` resource to the `cacti::install` class:

```
file { '/usr/share/cacti/cli/remove_device.php':
  ensure  => file,
  mode    => '0755',
  source  =>
      'puppet:///modules/packt_cacti/usr/share/cacti/cli/
    remove_device.php',
  require => Package['cacti'],
}
```

You can then add an `ensure` attribute to the `cacti::device` type:

```
define packt_cacti::device(
  $ensure='present',
  $ip,
  $ping_method='icmp',
{
  $cli = '/usr/share/cacti/cli'
  $search = "sed 1d | cut -f4- | grep -q '^${title}\$'"
  case $ensure {
  'present': {
    # existing cacti::device code goes here
  }
  'absent': {
    $remove = "${cli}/remove_device.php"
    $get_id = "${remove} --list-devices | awk -F'\\t'
       '\$4==\"${title}\" { print \$1 }'"
    exec { "remove-cacti-device-${name}":
       command => "${remove} --device-id=\$( ${get_id}
      )",
```

```
          path    => '/bin:/usr/bin',
          onlyif  => "${cli}/add_graphs.php --list-hosts |
              ${search}",
          require => Class[cacti],
        }
      }
    }
  }
```

Note that we took some liberties with the indentation here, so as to not break too many lines. This new `exec` resource is quite a mouthful, because the `remove_device.php` script requires the numeric ID of the device to be removed. This is retrieved with a `--list-devices` call that is piped to `awk`. To impair readability even more, some things such as double quotes, `$` signs, and backslashes must be escaped so that Puppet includes a valid `awk` script in the catalog.

Also note that the query for the sync state of this `exec` resource is identical to the one for the `add` resource, except that now it is used with the `onlyif` parameter: only take action *if* the device in question is still found in the configuration.

Dealing with complexity

The commands we implemented for the `packt_cacti::device` define are quite convoluted. At this level of complexity, shell one-liners become unwieldy for powering Puppet's resources. It gets even worse when handling the Cacti graphs; the `add_graphs.php` CLI script requires numeric IDs of not only the devices, but of the graphs as well. At this point, it makes sense to move the complexity out of the manifest and write wrapper scripts for the actual CLI. I will just sketch the implementation. The wrapper script will follow this general pattern.

```
#!/bin/bash
DEVICE_DESCR=$1
GRAPH_DESCR=$2
DEVICE_ID=` #scriptlet to retrieve numeric device ID`
GRAPH_ID=`  #scriptlet to retrieve numeric graph ID`
GRAPH_TYPE=`#scriptlet to determine the graph type`
/usr/share/cacti/cli/add_graphs.php \
  --graph-type=$GRAPH_TYPE \
  --graph-template-id=$GRAPH_ID \
  --host-id=$DEVICE_ID
```

With this, you can add a straightforward `graph` type:

```
define packt_cacti::graph(
  $device,
  $graph=$title
) {
  $add = '/usr/local/bin/cacti-add-graph'
  $find = '/usr/local/bin/cacti-find-graph'
  exec { "add-graph-${title}-to-${device}":
    command => "${add} '${device}' '${graph}'",
    path    => '/bin:/usr/bin',
    unless  => "${find} '${device}' '${graph}'",
  }
}
```

This also requires, an additional `cacti-find-graph` script. Adding this poses an additional challenge as the current CLI has no capabilities for listing configured graphs. There are many more functionalities that can be added to a `cacti` module, such as the management of Cacti's data sources and the ability to change options of the devices and, possibly, other objects that already exist in the configuration.

Such commodities are beyond the essentials and won't be detailed here. Let's look at some other parts for your exemplary `cacti` module instead.

Enhancing the agent through plugins

The reusable classes and defines give manifests that use your module much more expressive power. Installing and configuring Cacti now works concisely, and the manifest to do this becomes very readable and maintainable.

It's time to tap into the even more powerful aspect of modules: Puppet plugins. The different types of plugins are custom facts (which were discussed in Chapter 3, *A Peek into the Ruby Part of Puppet - Facts, Types, and Providers*), parser functions, resource types, and providers. All these plugins are stored in the modules on the master and get synchronized to all the agents. The agent will not use the parser functions (they are available to the users of `puppet apply` on the agent machine once they are synchronized, however); instead, the facts and resource types do most of their work on the agent. Let's concentrate on the types and providers for now; the other plugins will be discussed in dedicated sections later.

This section can be considered optional. Many users will never touch the code for any resource type or provider the manifests give you all the flexibility you will ever need. If you don't care for plugins, do skip ahead to the final sections about finding the Forge modules. On the other hand, if you are confident about your Ruby skills and would like to take advantage of them in your Puppet installations, read on to find the ways in which custom types and providers can help you.

While the custom resource types are functional on both the master and the agent, the provider will do all its work on the agent side. Although the resource types also perform mainly through the agent, they have one effect on the master; they enable manifests to declare resources of the type. The code not only describes what properties and parameters exist, but it can also include the validation and transformation code for the respective values. This part is invoked by the agent. Some resource types even do the synchronization and queries themselves, although there is usually at least one provider that takes care of this.

In the previous section, you implemented a defined type that did all its synchronization by wrapping some `exec` resources. By installing binaries and scripts through Puppet, you can implement almost any kind of functionality this way and extend Puppet without ever writing one plugin. This does have some disadvantages, however:

- The output is cryptic in the ideal case and overwhelming in the case of errors
- Puppet shells out to at least one external process per resource; and in many cases, multiple forks are required

In short, you pay a price, both in terms of usability and performance. Consider the `packt_cacti::device` type. For each declared resource, Puppet will have to run an `exec` resource's `unless` query on each run (or `onlyif` when `ensure => absent` is specified). This consists of one call to a PHP script (which can be expensive) as well as several core utilities that have to parse the output. On a Cacti server with dozens or hundreds of managed devices, these calls add up and make the agent spend a lot of time forking off and waiting for these child processes.

Consider a provider, on the other hand. It can implement an `instances` hook, which will create an internal list of configured Cacti devices once during initialization. This requires only one PHP call in total, and all the processing of the output can be done in the Ruby code directly inside the agent process. These savings alone will make each run much less expensive: resources that are already synchronized will incur no penalty, because no additional external commands need to be run.

Let's take a quick look at the agent output before we go ahead and implement a simple type/provider pair. The following is the output of the `cacti::device` type when it creates a device:

```
Notice:
/Stage[main]/Main/Node[agent]/Packt_cacti::Device[Agent_VM_Debian_7]/Exec[a
dd-cacti-device-Agent_VM_Debian_7]/returns: executed successfully
```

The native types express such actions in a much cleaner manner, such as the output from a `file` resource:

```
Notice:  /Stage[main]/Main/File[/usr/local/bin/cacti-search-graph]/ensure:
created
```

Replacing a defined type with a native type

The process of creating a custom resource type with a matching provider
(or several providers) is not easy. Let's go through the steps involved:

- Naming your type
- Creating the resource type's interface
- Designing sensible parameter hooks
- Using resource names
- Adding a provider
- Declaring management commands
- Implementing the basic functionality
- Allowing the provider to prefetch existing resources
- Making the type robust during provisioning

Naming your type

The first important difference between the native and defined types is the naming. There is no module namespacing for the custom types as you get with the defined types, which are manifest-based. Native types from all the installed modules mingle freely, if you will. They use plain names. It would, therefore, be unwise to call the native implementation of `packt_cacti::device` just `device` – this will easily clash with whatever notion of devices another module might have. The obvious choice for naming your first resource type is `cacti_device`.

The type must be completely implemented in
`packt_cacti/lib/puppet/type/cacti_device.rb`. All hooks and calls will be
enclosed in a `Type.newtype` block:

```
Puppet::Type.newtype(:cacti_device) do
  @doc = <<-EOD
    Manages Cacti devices.
    EOD
end
```

The documentation string in `@doc` should be considered mandatory, and it should be a bit
more substantial than this example. Consider including one or more example resource
declarations. Put all the further code pieces between the `EOD` terminator and the final `end`.

Creating the resource type's interface

First of all, the type should have the `ensure` property. Puppet's resource types have a
handy helper method that generates all the necessary type code for it through a simple
invocation:

`ensurable`

With this method call in the body of the type, you add the typical `ensure` property,
including all the necessary hooks. This line is all that is needed in the type code (actual
implementation will follow in the provider). Most properties and parameters require more
code, just the same as the `ip` parameter:

```
require 'ipaddr'
newparam(:ip) do
  desc "The IP address of the device."
  isrequired
  validate do |value|
    begin
      IPAddr.new(value)
    rescue ArgumentError
      fail "'#{value}' is not a valid IP address"
    end
  end
  munge do |value|
    value.downcase
  end
end
```

This should usually be an `ip` property instead, but the provider will rely on the Cacti CLI, which has no capability for changing the already configured devices. If the IP address was a property, such changes would be required in order to perform property-value synchronization.

As you can see, the IP address parameter code consists mostly of validation. Add the `require 'ipaddr'` line near the top of the file rather than inside the `Type.newtype` block.

The parameter is now available for the `cacti_device` resources, and the agent will even refuse to add devices whose IP addresses are not valid. This is helpful for users, because obvious typos in the addresses will be detected early. Let's implement the next parameter before we look at the `munge` hook more closely.

Designing sensible parameter hooks

Moving right along to the `ping_method` parameter, it accepts values only from a limited set, so validation is easy:

```
newparam(:ping_method) do
  desc "How the device's reachability is determined.
    One of `tcp` (default), `udp` or `icmp`."
  validate do |value|
    [ :tcp, :udp, :icmp ].include?(value.downcase.to_sym)
  end
  munge do |value|
    value.downcase.to_sym
  end
  defaultto :tcp
end
```

Looking at the `munge` blocks carefully, you will notice that they aim at unifying the input values. This is much less critical for the parameters than the properties, but if either of these parameters is changed to a property in a future release of your Cacti module, it will not try to sync a `ping_method` of `tcp` to `TCP`. The latter might appear if the users prefer uppercase in their manifest. Both values just become `:tcp` through munging. For the IP address, invoking `downcase` has an effect only for IPv6.

Beyond the scope of Puppet itself, the munging of a parameter's value is important as well. It allows Puppet to accept more convenient values than the subsystem being managed. For example, Cacti might not accept TCP as a value, but Puppet will, and it will do the right thing with it.

Using resource names

You need to take care of one final requirement: each Puppet resource type must declare a name variable or namevar, for short. This parameter will use the resource title from the manifest as its value, if the parameter itself is not specified for the resource. For example, the exec type has the command parameter for its namevar. You can either put the executable command into the resource title or explicitly declare the parameter:

```
exec { '/bin/true': }
# same effect:
exec { 'some custom name': command => '/bin/true' }
```

To mark one of the existing parameters as the name variable, call the isnamevar method in that parameter's body. If a type has a parameter called :name, it automatically becomes the name variable. This is a safe default.

```
newparam(:name) do
   desc "The name of the device."
   #isnamevar # → commented because automatically assumed
end
```

The resource type is now already usable inside a manifest:

```
cacti_device { 'eth0':
   ensure      => present,
   ip          => $::ipaddress,
   ping_method => 'icmp',
}
```

This code will get compiled into a catalog, but the agent will produce an error, due to the reason that there is no provider available.

Adding a provider

The resource type itself is ready for action, but it lacks a provider to do the actual work of inspecting the system and performing the synchronization. Let's build it step by step, just the same as the type. The name of the provider need not reflect the resource type it's for. Instead, it should contain a reference to the management approach it implements. Since your provider will rely on the Cacti CLI, name it `cli`. It's fine for multiple providers to share a name if they provide functionality to different types.

Create the skeleton structure in
`packt_cacti/lib/puppet/provider/cacti_device/cli.rb`:

```
Puppet::Type.type(:cacti_device).provide(
  :cli,
  :parent => Puppet::Provider
  ) do
end
```

Specifying `:parent => Puppet::Provider` is not necessary, actually.
`Puppet::Provider` is the default base class for the providers. If you write a couple of similar providers for a subsystem (each catering to a different resource type), all of which rely on the same toolchain, you might want to implement a base provider that becomes the parent for all the sibling providers.

For now, let's concentrate on putting together a self-sufficient `cli` provider for the `cacti_device` type. First of all, declare the commands that you are going to need.

Declaring management commands

Providers use the `commands` method to conveniently bind executables to Ruby identifiers:

```
commands :php => 'php'
commands :add_device => '/usr/share/cacti/cli/add_device.php'
commands :add_graphs => '/usr/share/cacti/cli/add_graphs.php'
commands :rm_device => '/usr/share/cacti/cli/remove_device.php'
```

You won't be invoking `php` directly. It's included here because declaring commands serves two purposes:

- You can conveniently call the commands through a generated method
- The provider will mark itself as `valid` only if all the commands are found

So, if the `php` CLI command is not found in Puppet's search path, Puppet will consider the provider to be dysfunctional. The user can determine this error condition quite quickly through Puppet's debug output.

Implementing the basic functionality

The basic functions of the provider can now be implemented in three instance methods. The names of these methods are not magic as such, but these are the methods that the default `ensure` property expects to be available (remember that you used the `ensurable` shortcut in the type code).

The first is the method that creates a resource if it does not exist yet. It must gather all the resource parameter's values and build an appropriate call to `add_device.php`:

```
def create
  args = []
  args << "--description=#{resource[:name]}"
  args << "--ip=#{resource[:ip]}"
  args << "--ping_method=#{resource[:ping_method]}"
  add_device(*args)
end
```

 Don't quote the parameter values as you would quote them on the command-line. Puppet takes care of this for you. It also escapes any quotes that are in the arguments, so in this case, Cacti will receive any quotes for inclusion in the configuration. For example, this will lead to an incorrect title.

```
args << "--description='#{resource[:name]}'"
```

The provider must also be able to remove or `destroy` an entity:

```
def destroy
  rm_device("--device-id=#{@property_hash[:id]}")
end
```

The `property_hash` variable is an instance member of the provider. Each resource gets its specific provider instance. Read on to learn how it gets initialized to include the device's ID number.

Before we get to that, let's add the final provider method in order to implement the `ensure` property. This is a query method that the agent uses to determine whether a resource is already present:

```
def exists?
  self.class.instances.find do |provider|
    provider.name == resource[:name]
  end
end
```

The `ensure` property relies on the provider class method `instances` in order to get a list of `providers` for all the entities on the system. It compares each of them with the `resource` attribute, which is the resource type instance for which this current provider instance is performing the work. If this is rather confusing, please refer to the diagram in the next section.

Allowing the provider to prefetch existing resources

The `instances` method is truly special - it implements the prefetching of the system resources during the provider initialization. You have to add it to the provider yourself. Some subsystems are not suitable for the mass-fetching of all the existing resources (such as the `file` type). These providers don't have an `instances` method. Enumerating the Cacti devices, on the other hand, is quite possible:

```
def self.instances
  return @instances ||= add_graphs("--list-hosts").
    split("\n").
    drop(1).
    collect do |line|
      fields = line.split(/\t/, 4)
      Puppet.debug "prefetching cacti_device #{fields[3]}
      " +
              "with ID #{fields[0]}"
      new(:ensure => :present,
            :name => fields[3],
             :id => fields[0])
    end
end
```

The ensure value of the provider instance reflects the current state. The method creates instances for the resources that are found on the system, so for these, the value is always present. Also note that the result of the method is cached in the @instances class member variable. This is important, because the exists? method calls instances, which can happen a lot.

Puppet requires another method to perform proper prefetching. The mass-fetching you implemented through instances supplies the agent with a list of provider instances that represent the entities found on the system. From the master, the agent received a list of the resource type instances. However, Puppet has not yet built a relation between the resources (type instances) and providers. You need to add a prefetch method to the provider class in order to make this happen:

```
def self.prefetch(resources)
   instances.each do |provider|
      if res = resources[provider.name]
         res.provider = provider
      end
   end
end
```

The agent passes the cacti_device resources as a hash, with the resource title as the respective key. This makes lookups very simple (and quick).

This completes the cli provider for the cacti_device type. You can now replace your cacti::device resources with the cacti_device instances to enjoy improved performance and cleaner agent output:

```
node "agent" {
   include cacti
   cacti_device { 'Puppet test agent (Debian 7)":
      ensure => present,
      ip     => $::ipaddress,
   }
}
```

Note that, unlike your defined type cacti::device, a native type will not assume a default value of present for its ensure property. Therefore, you have to specify it for any cacti_device resource. Otherwise, Puppet will only manage the properties of the resources that already exist and not care about whether the entity exists or not. In the particular case of cacti_device, this will never do anything, because there are no other properties (only parameters).

You can refer to `Chapter 6`, *The Puppet Beginners Advanced Parts*, on how to use resource defaults to save you from the repetition of the `ensure => present` specification.

Making the type robust during provisioning

There is yet another small issue with the `packt_cacti` module. It is self-sufficient and handles both the installation and configuration of Cacti. However, this means that during Puppet's first run, the `cacti` package and its CLI will not be available, and the agent will correctly determine that the `cli` provider is not yet suitable. Since it is the only provider for the `cacti_device` type, any resource of this type that is synchronized before the `cacti` package will fail.

In the case of the defined type `packt_cacti::device`, you just added the `require` metaparameters to the inner resources. To achieve the same end for the native type instances, you can work with the `autorequire` feature. Just as the files automatically depend on their containing directory, the Cacti resources should depend on the successful synchronization of the `cacti` package. Add the following block to the `cacti_device` type:

```
autorequire :package do
  catalog.resource(:package, 'cacti')
end
```

Enhancing Puppet's system knowledge through facts

When facts were introduced in `Chapter 3`, *A Peek into the Ruby Part of Puppet - Facts, Types, and Providers*, you got a small tour of the process of creating your own custom facts. We hinted at modules at that point, and now, we can take a closer look at how the fact code is deployed, using the example of the `Cacti` module. Let's focus on native Ruby facts - they are more portable than the external facts. As the latter are easy to create, there is no need to discuss them in depth here.

For details on external facts, you can refer to the online documentation on custom facts on the Puppet Labs site at `http://docs.puppetlabs.com/facter/latest/custom_facts.html#external-facts`.

Facts are part of the Puppet plugins that a module can contain, just as the types and providers from the previous sections. They belong in the `lib/facter/` subtree. For users of the `cacti` module, it might be helpful to learn which graph templates are available on a given Cacti server (once the graph management is implemented, that is). The complete list can be passed through a fact. The following code in `packt_cacti/lib/facter/cacti_graph_templates.rb` will do just this job:

```
Facter.add(:cacti_graph_templates) do
  setcode do
    cmd = '/usr/share/cacti/cli/add_graphs.php'
    Facter::Core::Execution.exec("#{cmd} --list-graph-
    templates").
      split("\n").
      drop(1).
      collect do |line|
        line.split(/\t/)[1]
      end
  end
end
```

The code will call the CLI script, skip its first line of output, and join the values from the second column of each remaining line in a list. Manifests can access this list through the global `$cacti_graph_templates` variable, just the same as any other fact.

Refining the interface of your module through custom functions

Functions can be of great help in keeping your manifest clean and maintainable, and some tasks cannot even be implemented without resorting to a Ruby function.

A frequent use of the custom functions (especially in Puppet 3) is input validation. You can do this in the manifest itself, but it can be a frustrating exercise because of the limitations of the language. The resulting Puppet DSL code can be hard to read and maintain. The `stdlib` module comes with the `validate_X` functions for many basic data types, such as `validate_bool`. Typed parameters in Puppet 4 and later versions make this more convenient and natural, because for the supported variable types, no validation function is needed anymore.

As with all the plugins, the functions need not be specific to the module's domain, and they instantly become available for all the manifests. A case in point is the `packt_cacti` module that can use the validation functions for the `packt_cacti::device` parameters. Checking whether a string contains a valid IP address is not at all specific to Cacti. On the other hand, checking whether `ping_method` is one of those that Cacti recognizes is not that generic.

To see how it works, let's just implement a function that does the job of the `validate` and `munge` hooks from the custom `cacti_device` type for the IP address parameter of `packt_cacti::device`. This should fail the compilation if the address is invalid; otherwise, it should return the unified address value:

```
module Puppet::Parser::Functions
  require 'ipaddr'
  newfunction(:cacti_canonical_ip, :type => :rvalue) do |args|
    ip = args[0]
    begin
      IPAddr.new(ip)
    rescue ArgumentError
      raise "#{@resource.ref}: invalid IP address '#{ip}'"
    end
    ip.downcase
  end
end
```

In the exception message, `@resource.ref` is expanded to the textual reference of the offending resource type instance, such as `Packt_cacti::Device[Edge Switch 03]`.

The following example illustrates the use of the function in the simple version of `cacti::device` without the `ensure` parameter:

```
define packt_cacti::device($ip) {
  $cli = '/usr/share/cacti/cli'
  $c_ip = cacti_canonical_ip(${ip})
  $options = "--description='${name}' --ip='${c_ip}'"
  exec { "add-cacti-device-${name}":
    command => "${cli}/add_device.php ${options}",
    require => Class[cacti],
  }
}
```

The manifest will then fail to compile if an IP address has (conveniently) transposed digits:

```
ip => '912.168.12.13'
```

IPv6 addresses will be converted to all lowercase letters.

 Puppet 4 introduced a more powerful API for defining the custom functions. Refer to Chapter 6, *The Puppet Beginners Advanced Parts*, to learn about its advantages.

Making your module portable across platforms

Sadly, our Cacti module is very specific to the Debian package. It expects to find the CLI at a certain place and the Apache configuration snippet at another. These locations are most likely specific to the Debian package. It would be useful for the module to work on the Red Hat derivatives as well.

The first step is to get an overview of the differences by performing a manual installation. I chose to test this with a virtual machine running Fedora 18. The basic installation is identical to Debian, except using yum instead of apt-get, of course. Puppet will automatically do the right thing here. The puppet::install class also contains a CLI file, though. The Red Hat package installs the CLI in /var/lib/cacti/cli, rather than /usr/share/cacti/cli.

If the module is supposed to support both platforms, the target location for the remove_device.php script is no longer fixed. Therefore, it's best to deploy the script from a central location in the module, while the target location on the agent system becomes a module parameter, if you will. Such values are customarily gathered in a params class:

```
# .../packt_cacti/manifests/params.pp
class packt_cacti::params {
  case $osfamily {
    'Debian': {
      $cli_path = '/usr/share/cacti/cli'
    }
    'RedHat': {
      $cli_path = '/var/lib/cacti/cli'
    }
    default: {
```

```
            fail "the cacti module does not yet support the
            ${osfamily}
              platform"
        }
      }
    }
```

It is best to fail the compilation for unsupported agent platforms. Users will have to remove the declaration of the `cacti` class from their module, rather than have Puppet try untested installation steps that most likely will not work (this might concern Gentoo or a BSD variant).

Classes that need to access the variable value must include the `params` class:

```
class packt_cacti::install {
    include pack_cacti::params
    file { 'remove_device.php':
      ensure => file,
      path    =>
        "${packt_cacti::params::cli_path}/remove_device.php',
      source =>
      'puppet:///modules/packt_cacti/cli/remove_device.php',
      mode    => '0755',
    }
}
```

Similar transformations will be required for the `cacti::redirect` class and the `cacti::config` class. Just add more variables to the `params` class. This is not limited to the manifests, either; the facts and providers must behave in accordance with the agent platform as well.

You will often see that the `params` class is inherited rather than included:

```
class packt_cacti(
    $redirect = ${packt_cacti::params::redirect}
) inherits packt_cacti::params{
    # ...
}
```

This is done because an `include` statement in the class body won't allow the use of variable values from the `params` class as the class parameter's default values, such as the `$redirect` parameter in this example.

The portability practices are often not required for your own custom modules. In the ideal case, you won't use them on more than one platform. The practice should be considered mandatory if you intend to share them on the Forge, though. For most of your Puppet needs, you will not want to write modules anyway, but download existing solutions from the Forge instead.

 In Puppet 4.9 and later versions, the params class pattern will no longer be necessary to ship the default parameter values. There is a new data binding mechanism instead. This mechanism is explained in Chapter 8, *Separation of Code and Data with Hiera*.

Finding helpful Forge modules

Using the web interface at http://forge.puppetlabs.com is very straightforward. By filling the search form with the name of the software, system, or service you need to manage, you will usually get a list of very fitting modules often with just your search term as their name. In fact, for common terms, the number of available modules can be overwhelming.

You can get immediate feedback about the maturity and popularity of each module. A module is being actively used and maintained if:

- It has a score close to 5
- It has a version number that indicates releases past 1.0.0 (or even 0.1.0)
- Its most recent release was not too long ago, perhaps less than half a year
- It has a significant number of downloads

The latter three numbers can vary a lot though, depending on the number of features that the module implements and how widespread its subject is. Even more importantly, just because a particular module gets much attention and regular contributions, it does necessarily mean that it is the best choice for your situation.

You are encouraged to evaluate less trafficked modules as well - you can unearth some hidden gems this way. The next section details some deeper indicators of quality for you to take into consideration.

If you cannot, or don't want to, spend too much time digging for the best module, you can also just refer to the sidebar with the **Puppet Supported** and **Puppet Approved** modules. All modules that are featured in these categories have got a seal of quality from Puppet Labs.

Identifying module characteristics

When navigating to a module's details in the Forge, you are presented with its README file. An empty or very sparse documentation speaks of little care taken by the module author. A sample manifest in the README file is often a good starting point in order to put a module to work quickly.

If you are looking for a module that will enhance your agents through additional resource types and providers, look for the **Types** tab on the module details page. It can also be enlightening to click on the **Project URL** link near the top of the module description. This usually leads to GitHub. Here, you can not only conveniently browse the plugins in the lib/ subtree, but also get a feel of how the module's manifests are structured.

Another sign of a carefully maintained module are unit tests. These are found in the spec/ subtree. This tree does exist for most of the Forge modules. It tends to be devoid of actual tests, though. There may be test code files for all the classes and the defined types that are part of the module's manifest; these are typically in the spec/classes/ and spec/defines/ subdirectories, respectively. For plugins, there will ideally be unit tests in spec/unit/ and spec/functions/.

Some README files of the modules contain a small greenish tag saying **build passing**. This can turn red on occasions, stating **build failing**. These modules use the Travis CI through GitHub, so they are likely to have at least a few unit tests.

Summary

All the development in Puppet should be done in modules, and each such module should serve as specific a purpose as possible. Most modules comprise only manifests. This suffices to provide very effective and readable node manifests that clearly and concisely express their intent by including aptly named classes and instantiating defined types.

Modules can also contain Puppet plugins in the form of resource types and providers, parser functions, or facts. All of these are usually Ruby code. External facts can be written in any language, though. Writing your own types and providers is not required, but it can boost your performance and management flexibility.

It is not necessary to write all your modules yourself. On the contrary, it's advisable to rely on the open source modules from the Puppet Forge as much as possible. The Puppet Forge is an ever-growing collection of helpful code for virtually all the systems and software that Puppet can manage. In particular, the modules that are curated by Puppet Labs are usually of very high quality. As with any open source software, you are more than welcome to add any missing requirements to the modules yourself.

After this broad view on Puppet's larger building blocks, Chapter 6, *The Puppet Beginners Advanced Parts*, narrows the scope a little. Now that you have the tools to structure and compose a manifest code base, you will learn some refined techniques in order to elegantly solve some distinct problems with Puppet.

6

The Puppet Beginners Advanced Parts

After our in-depth discussions on both the manifest structure elements (class and define) and encompassing structure (modules), you are in a great position to write manifests for all of your agents. Make sure that you get Forge modules that will allow them to do your work for you. Then go ahead and add site-specific modules that implement Forge modules to your needs. Finally, you will have composite classes for the node blocks to be used, or rather, included.

These concepts are quite a bit to take in. It's now time to decelerate a bit, lean back, and tackle simpler code structures and ideas. You are about to learn some techniques that you are not going to need every day. They can make difficult scenarios much easier, though. So, it might be a good idea to come back to this chapter again after you have spent some time in the field. You might find that some of your designs can be simplified with these tools.

Specifically, these are the techniques that will be presented:

- Building dynamic configuration files
- Managing file snippets
- Using virtual resources
- Cross-node configuration with exported resources
- Setting defaults for resource parameters
- Avoiding antipatterns

Building dynamic configuration files

In the introduction, I stated that the techniques that you are now learning are not frequently required. That was true, except for this one topic. Templates are actually a cornerstone of configuration management with Puppet.

Templates are an alternative way to manage configuration files, or any files really. You have synchronized files from the master to an agent that handled some Apache configuration settings. These are not templates, technically. They are merely static files that have been prepared and are ready for carbon copying.

These static files suffice in many situations, but sometimes, you will want the master to manage very specific configuration values for each agent. These values can be quite individual. For example, an Apache server usually requires a `MaxClients` setting. Appropriate values depend on many aspects, including hardware specifications and characteristics of the web application that is being run. It would be impractical to prepare all possible choices as distinct files in the module.

Learning the template syntax

Templates make short work of such scenarios. With Puppet 4 EPP (embedded Puppet) templates were introduced. The older ERB (embedded Ruby) templates are still available and fully functional. If you know your way around PHP or JSP, you will quickly get the hang of EPP or ERB Puppet templates. The following EPP template will produce `Hello,world!` three times:

```
<% [1,2,3].each  |$p| { %>
Hello, world!
<% } %>
```

The following ERB template does the same:

```
<% (1 .. 3).each  do %>
Hello, world!
<% end %>
```

This template will also produce lots of empty lines, because the text between the `<%` and `%>` tags gets removed from the output but the final line breaks do not. To make the EPP engine do just that, change the closing tag to `-%>`:

```
<% [1,2,3].each |$p| { -%>
Hello, world!
<% } -%>
```

This example is not very helpful for configuration files, of course. To include dynamic values in the output, enclose Ruby expressions in a `<%=tag` pair:

```
<% [1,2,3].each  |$index|  { -%>
Hello, world #<%= $index %> !
<% } -%>
```

Now, the iterator value is part of each line of the output. You can also use member variables that are prefixed with the `$` sign and use the full namespace to the variable.

These variables are populated with the values from the Puppet manifest variables:

```
<IfModule mpm_worker_module>
ServerLimit         <%= $apache::apache_server_limit %>
StartServers        <%= $apache::apache_start_servers %>
MaxClients          <%= $apache::apache_max_clients %>
</IfModule>
<% $apache::apache_ports.each  |$port| { -%>
Listen <%= $port %>
NameVirtualHost *:<%= $port %>
<% } -%>
```

Variables that are used in a template must be defined in the same scope or scopes from which the template is used. The next section explains how this works.

In Puppet 3.x, variable values are mostly strings, arrays, or hashes. To write efficient templates, it is helpful to occasionally glance at the methods available for the respective Ruby classes. In Puppet 4, variables have more diverse values.

There are several ways to use Puppet variables in ERB templates:

- Prefixing the variable with the @ sign: This means that the variable is global, or it was defined in the same class where the template is used. This works with Puppet 2.7, Puppet 3, and Puppet 4
- Using the `scope.lookupvar('variablewithscopename')` function: This allows you to refer to any variable in any class of the module. Please do not look up variables in other modules; it will build an invisible dependency on the other module. The syntax works with Puppet 2, Puppet 3, and Puppet 4
- Using `scope['variablewithscope']`: In Puppet 3, the scope hash can be used directly. The behavior is similar to `scope.lookupvar`. This will work with Puppet 3 and Puppet 4

Using templates in practice

Templates have their own place in modules. You can place them freely in the `templates/` subtree of the module. The `epp` function locates them using a simple descriptor:

```
epp('cacti/apache/cacti.conf.epp')
```

This expression evaluates the content of the template found in `modules/cacti/templates/apache/cacti.conf.epp`. The first path element (without a leading slash) is the module name. The rest of the path gets translated to the `templates/` tree in the module. The function is commonly used to generate the value of a `file` resource's `content` property:

```
file { '/etc/apache2/conf.d/cacti.conf':
  content => epp('cacti/apache/cacti.conf.epp'),
}
```

Many templates expect some variables to be defined in their scope. The easiest way to make sure that this happens is to wrap the respective `file` resource in a parameterized container. Files that are **singletons** with a well-known name, such as `/etc/ssh/sshd_config`, should be managed through a parameterized class. Configuration items that can inhabit multiple files, such as `/etc/logrotate.d/*` or `/etc/apache2/conf.d/*`, are well suited to being wrapped in defined types:

```
define logrotate::conf(
  String $pattern,
  Integer $max_days=7,
  Array $options=[]
) {
  file { "/etc/logrotate.d/$name":
    ensure  => file,
    mode    => '0644',
    content => epp('logrotate/config-snippet.epp',
      {
        'pattern'  => $pattern,
        'max_days' => $max_days,
        'options'  => $options,
      },)
  }
}
```

There is one main difference between EPP templates in classes compared to EPP templates in defines. EPP templates in classes can directly use the class variables with the namespace. A defined resource type does not have a fixed namespace. Therefore, it is required to add a mapping hash to the `epp` function, where we specify the variable inside the template and the corresponding variable inside the define.

Afterwards, one can use the variables directly inside the template ($pattern, $max_days, $options).

For a quick and dirty string transformation of your data, you can also use the inline_epp function in your manifest. This is often found on the right-hand side of a variable assignment:

```
$comma_seperated_list = inline_epp('<%= $my_class::my_array * "," %>')
```

This example assumes that the $my_array Puppet variable in the my_class class holds an array value.

Avoiding performance bottlenecks from templates

When using templates, both through the epp and inline_epp functions, be aware that each invocation implies a performance penalty for your Puppet master. During the compilation of the catalog, Puppet must initialize the EPP engine for any template it encounters. The EPP evaluation happens in an individual environment that is derived from the respective scope of the epp function invocation.

It is, therefore, not even important how complex your templates are. If your manifest requires frequent expansion of a very short template, it generates an enormous overhead for each initialization. Especially in the case of an easy inline_epp function, such as the one mentioned previously, it can be worthwhile to invest some more effort into creating a parser function instead, as seen in Chapter 5, *Combining Classes, Configuration Files, and Extensions into Modules*. A function can perform variable value transformation without incurring the cumulative penalty.

On the bright side, using templates is quite economic for the agent, who receives the whole textual file content right inside the catalog. There is no need to make an additional call to the master and retrieve file metadata. On a high-latency network, this can be a noticeable saving.

There is no silver bullet here. Don't let the performance implications deter you from turning specific configuration files into templates. Template-based solutions will often make your module more maintainable, which will usually offset performance implications; hardware is constantly getting cheaper, after all. Just don't be wasteful with frequent (and simple) expansions.

Managing file snippets

The next technique that we are going to discuss helps you solve conflicts in your manifests and build some elegant solutions in special situations. This mostly refers to configuration files where one is either not able to manage the whole file or where a file is constructed from different subclasses.

Puppet offers several ways to accomplish this:

- Single line
- Single entry in a section
- Building from multiple snippets
- Other resource types

How do you deal with a configuration file, where a user may add additional content? What we have seen so far is management of complete configuration files, where changes will get reset. But think about the users .bashrc file, where the system administrator wants to ensure that the user is making use of a specific proxy.

> Normally, one can specify this globally in a /etc/profile.d/ snippet. This is more meant to be a showcase.

Puppet has a specific resource type which is able to manage a single line entry in a configuration file: the file_line resource type. This resource type is not a core resource type but is delivered by stdlib module.

```
file_line { 'user admin proxy':
  ensure   => present,
  path     => '/home/admin/.bashrc',
  line     => 'export
  http_proxy=http://proxy.domain.com:3127',
}
```

In the previous example, the line will be added at the bottom of the file, if it is missing. If the line is already available, Puppet will not change the file.

Please remember that the `file_line` resource type expects that the file is already present on the system. If one is unsure about this, it is best practice to also manage the existence of the file without specifying content or source:

```
file { '/home/admin/.bashrc':
  ensure => file,
  owner  => 'admin',
  group  => 'admin',
  mode   => '0644',
}
```

Single entry in a section

But what if one needs to configure a line within a configuration file which consists of sections? In this case, it is not a good idea to add the line at the bottom of the file.

This is where the `ini_setting` resource type will be helpful. This resource type is not part of Puppet core, but is shipped with `puppetlabs-inifile` module.

```
ini_setting { 'puppet agent report':
  ensure  => present,
  path    => '/etc/puppetlabs/puppet/puppet.conf',
  section => 'agent',
  setting => 'report',
  value   => 'true',
}
```

The previous example will check whether the agent section has an entry report = `true` and add it if it is missing. If the whole section is not yet there, it will also add the section. If the whole file is missing, the `ini_setting` resource type will also create the file.

Normally, the `ini_setting` assumes that section names are put into brackets and that the = sign is used as a setting-value separator.

The resource type allows the adoption of `section_prefix` and `section_suffix` and `key_value_separator`.

```
ini_setting { 'ssh config host default':
  ensure              => present,
  path                => '/etc/ssh/ssh_config',
  section             => 'Host *',
  section_prefix      => '',
  section_suffix      => '',
  key_value_separator => ' ',
  setting             => 'HashKnownHosts',
```

```
   value                 => 'true',
 }
```

This will produce the following output:

```
Host *
HashKnownHosts true
```

But managing all single entries in `ssh_config` file is very ineffective, as one must provide all single entries within single recourse type declarations. In this specific case, it is feasible to build the configuration file from snippets.

Building from multiple snippets

There is one main difference between building a file from snippets compared to the `file_line` and `ini_setting` resource type. The latter two just manage single entries in a file, whereas managing a file from snippets manages the complete configuration file.

This is very useful if one does not know beforehand how many entries are needed. For example, dynamically scaling haproxy backends or adding backup entries for a database server where the number of databases is yet unknown.

The most common solution for file snippets is the `puppetlabs-concat` module. The `concat` module needs at least one `no-noop` run, as it must manage the `concat` script on the nodes. This script is needed to build the final configuration file.

First, it is required to mention to `concat` which file it is about to manage:

```
concat { 'ssh config':
  ensure => present,
  path   => '/etc/ssh/ssh_config',
}
```

This prepares `concat` to be able to build the file from `concat_fragments`. All fragments should be put into a specific order:

```
concat::fragment { 'ssh_config header':
  target  => 'ssh config',
  content => "# Managed by Pupept\n",
  order   => '01',
}
concat::fragment { 'default host':
  target  => 'ssh config',
```

```
    source =>
'puppet:///modules/<modulename>/ssh_config_default host',
    order => '10',
}
```

Using virtual resources

The next technique that we are going to discuss helps you solve conflicts in your manifests and build some elegant solutions in special situations.

Remember the uniqueness constraint that was introduced in Chapter 1, *Writing Your First Manifests*, any resource must be declared at most once in a manifest. There cannot be two classes or defined type instances that declare the same `file`, `package`, or any other type of resource. Each resource must have a unique type/name combination. This applies to instances of defined types as well as native resources.

This can pose issues when multiple modules need a common resource, such as an installed package, or perhaps even independent settings in the same configuration file. A component class for such resources, as introduced in Chapter 4, *Combining Resources in Classes and Defined Types*, will resolve basic conflicts of this kind. It can be included an arbitrary number of times in the same manifest.

This can be impractical when the number of shared resources is fairly large. Imagine that you find yourself in a situation where a large number of different Puppet nodes require software from a significant set of `yum` repositories. Puppet will happily manage the repository configuration on the agents through its `yumrepo` type. However, you don't actually want all these repositories configured on every last machine they do incur maintenance overhead, after all. It would, instead, be desirable for each node to automatically receive the configuration for all repositories it requires for its packages, but not more.

When solving this using component classes, you would wrap each repository in a distinct class. The class names should closely resemble (and most likely contain) the name of the respective repositories:

```
class yumrepos::team_ninja_stable {
  yumrepo { 'team_ninja_stable':
    ensure => present,
    ...
  }
}
```

Package resources that rely on one or more such repositories will need to be accompanied by appropriate `include` statements:

```
include yumrepos::team_ninja_stable
include yumrepos::team_wizard_experimental
package { 'doombunnies':
  ensure  => installed,
  require => [
    Class['yumrepos::team_ninja_stable'],
    Class['yumrepos::team_wizard_experimental']
  ],
}
```

This is possible, but it is less than ideal. Puppet does offer an alternative way to avoid duplicate resource declarations in the form of virtual resources. It allows you to add a resource declaration to your manifest without adding the resource to the actual catalog. The virtual resource must be **realized** or **collected** for this purpose. As with class inclusion, this realization of virtual resources can happen arbitrarily in the same manifest.

Our previous example can, therefore, use a simpler structure with just one class to declare all the `yum` repositories as virtual resources with tag parameter set:

```
class yumrepos::all {
  @yumrepo { 'tem_ninja_stable':
    ensure => present,
    tag    => 'stable',
  }
  @yumrepo { 'team_wizard_experimantel':
    ensure => present,
    tag    => 'experimental',
  }
}
```

The @ prefix marks the `yumrepo` resources as virtual. This class can be safely included by all nodes. It will not affect the catalog until the resources are realized:

```
realize(Yumrepo['team_ninja_stable'])
realize(Yumrepo['team_wizard_experimental'])
package { 'doombunnies':
  ensure  => installed,
  require => [
    Yumrepo['team_ninja_stable'],
    Yumrepo['team_wizard_experimental'],
  ],
}
```

The `realize` function converts the referenced virtual resources to real ones, which get added to the catalog. Granted, this is not much better than the previous code that relied on the component classes. The virtual resources do make the intent clearer, at least. Realizing them is less ambiguous than some `include` statements; a class can contain many resources and even more `include` statements.

 This `define` structure is actually possible with component classes as well. The class names can be passed as a parameter or from a central data structure. The `include` function will accept variable values for class names.

Realizing resources more flexibly using collectors

Instead of invoking the `realize` function, you can also rely on a different syntactic construct, which is the `collector`:

```
Yumrepo<| title == 'team_ninja_stable' |>
```

This is more flexible than the function call at the cost of a slight performance penalty. It can be used as a reference to the realized resource(s) in certain contexts. For example, you can add ordering constraints with the chaining operator:

```
Yumrepo<| title == 'team_ninja_stable' |> -> Class['...']
```

It is even possible to change values of resource attributes during collection. There is a whole section dedicated to such overrides later in this chapter.

As the collector is based on an expression, you can conveniently realize a whole range of resources. This can be quite dynamic sometimes, you will create virtual resources that are already being realized by a rather indiscriminate collector. Let's look at a common example:

```
User<| |>
```

With no expression, the collection encompasses all virtual resources of the given type. This allows you to collect them all, without worrying about their explicit titles or attributes. This might seem redundant, because then it makes no sense to declare the resources as virtual in the first place. However, keep in mind that the collector might appear in some select manifests only, while the virtual resources can be safely added to all your nodes.

To be a little more selective, it can be useful to group virtual resources based on their **tags**. We haven't discussed tags yet. Each resource is tagged with several identifiers. Each tag is just a simple string. You can tag a resource manually by defining the `tag` metaparameter:

```
file { '/etc/sysctl.conf':
  ensure => file,
  tag    => 'security',
}
```

The named tag is then added to the resource. Puppet implicitly tags all resources with the name of the declaring class, the containing module, and a range of other useful meta information. For example, if your user module divides the `user` resources into classes such as `administrators`, `developers`, `qa`, and other roles, you can make certain nodes or classes select all users of a given role with a collection based on the class name tag:

```
User<| tag == 'developers' |>
```

Note that the tags actually form an array. The `==` comparison will look for the presence of the `developers` element in the `tag` array in this context. Have a look at another example to make this more clear:

```
@user { 'felix':
  ensure => present,
  groups => [ 'power', 'sys' ],
}
User<| groups == 'sys' |>
```

This way, you can collect all users who are members of the `sys` group.

If you prefer function calls over the more cryptic collector syntax, you can keep using the `realize` function alongside collectors. This works without issues. Remember that each resource can be realized multiple times, even in both ways, simultaneously.

If you are wondering, the manifest for a given agent can only realize virtual resources that are declared inside this same agent's manifest. Virtual resources do not leak into other manifests. Consequently, there can be no deliberate transfer of resources from one manifest to another, either. However, there is yet another concept that allows such an exchange; this is described in the next section.

Cross-node configuration with exported resources

Puppet is commonly used to configure whole clusters of servers or HPC workers. Any configuration management system makes this task very efficient in comparison to manual care. Manifests can be shared between similar nodes. Configuration items that require individual customization per node are modeled individually. The whole process is very natural and direct.

On the other hand, there are certain configuration tasks that do not lend themselves well to the paradigm of the central definition of all states. For example, a cluster setup might include the sharing of a generated key or registering IP addresses of peer nodes as they become available. An automatic setup should include an exchange of such shared information. Puppet can help out with this as well.

This is a very good fit. It saves a metalayer, because you don't need to implement the setup of an information exchange system in Puppet. The sharing is secure, relying on Puppet's authentication and encryption infrastructure. There is logging and central control over the deployment of the shared configuration. Puppet retains its role as the central source for all system details; it serves as a hub for a secure exchange of information.

Exporting and collecting resources

Puppet approaches the problem of sharing configuration information among multiple agent nodes by way of exported resources. The concept is simple. The manifest of **node A** can contain one or more resources that are purely virtual and not for realization in the manifest of this **node A**. Other nodes, such as **B** and **C**, can import some or all of these resources. Then, the resources become part of the catalogs of these remote nodes.

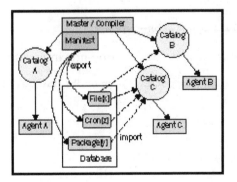

The syntax to import and export resources is very similar to that of virtual resources. An exported resource is declared by prepending the resource type name with two @ characters:

```
@@file { 'my-app-psk':
  ensure  => file,
  path    => '/etc/my-app/psk',
  content => 'nwNFgzsn9n3sDfnFANfoinaAEF',
  tag     => 'cluster02',
}
```

The importing manifests collect these resources using an expression, which is again similar to the collection of virtual resources, but with double-angled brackets, < and >:

```
File <<| tag == 'cluster02' |>>
```

Tags are a very common way to take fine-grained control over the distribution of such exported resources.

Configuring the master to store exported resources

The only recommendable way to enable support for exported resources is PuppetDB. It is a REST API that stores different kinds of data that the Puppet master deals with during regular operation in a PostgreSQL database. This includes catalog requests from agents (including their valuable facts), reports from catalog applications, and exported resources.

Chapter 2, *Puppet Server and Agents*, detailed a manual installation of the master. Let's add the PuppetDB with more style through Puppet! On the Forge, you will find a convenient module that will make this easy:

```
puppet module install puppetlabs-puppetdb
```

On the master node, the setup now becomes a one-line invocation:

```
puppet apply -e 'include puppetdb, puppetdb::master::config'
```

As our test master uses a nonstandard SSL certificate that is named `master.example.net` (instead of its FQDN), it must be configured for `puppetdb` as well:

```
include puppetdb
class { 'puppetdb::master::config':
        puppetdb_server => 'master.example.net',
    }
```

The ensuing catalog run is quite impressive. Puppet installs the PostgreSQL backend, the Jetty server, and the actual PuppetDB package, and it configures everything and starts the services up all in one go. After applying this short manifest, you have added a complex piece of infrastructure to your Puppet setup. You can now use exported resources for a variety of helpful tasks.

Exporting SSH host keys

For homegrown interactions between clustered machines, SSH can be an invaluable tool. File transfer and the remote execution of arbitrary commands is easily possible thanks to the ubiquitous `sshd` service. For security reasons, each host generates a unique key in order to identify itself. Of course, such public key authentication systems can only really work with a trust network, or the presharing of public keys.

Puppet can do the latter quite nicely:

```
@@sshkey { $::facts['networking']['fqdn']:
  host_aliases => $::facts['networking']['hostname'],
  key          => $::facts['sshecdsakey'],
  tag          => 'san-nyc'
}
```

Interested nodes collect keys with the known pattern:

```
Sshkey<<| tag == 'san-nyc' |>>
```

Now, SSH servers can be authenticated through the respective keys that Puppet safely stores in its database. As always, the Puppet master is the fulcrum of security.

As a matter of fact, some `ssh` modules from the Puppet Forge will use this kind of construct to do this work for you.

Managing hosts files locally

Many sites can rely on a local DNS infrastructure. Resolving names to local IP addresses is easy with such setups. However, small networks, or sites that consist of many independent clusters with little shared infrastructure, will have to rely on names in /etc/hosts instead.

You can maintain a central hosts file per network cell, or you can make Puppet maintain each entry in each hosts file separately. The latter approach has some advantages:

- Changes are automatically distributed through the Puppet agent network
- Puppet copes with unmanaged lines in the hosts files

A manually maintained registry is prone to becoming outdated every once in a while. It will also obliterate local additions in any hosts files on the agent machines.

The manifest implementation of the superior approach with exported resources is very similar to the sshkey example from the previous section:

```
@@host { $::facts['networking']['fqdn']:
  ip            => $::facts['networking']['ipaddress'],
  host_aliases => [ $::facts['networking']['hostname'] ],
  tag           => 'nyc-site',
}
```

This is the same principle, only now, each node exports its $ipaddress fact value alongside its name and not a public key. The import also works the same way:

```
Host<<| tag == 'nyc-site' |>>
```

Automating custom configuration items

Do you remember the Cacti module that you created during the previous chapter? It makes it very simple to configure all monitored devices in the manifest of the Cacti server. However, as this is possible, wouldn't it be even better if each node in your network was registered automatically with Cacti? It's simple: make the devices export their respective cacti_device resources for the server to collect:

```
@@cacti_device { $::facts['networking']['fqdn']:
  ensure => present,
  ip     => $::facts['networking']['ipaddress'],
  tag    => 'nyc-site',
}
```

The Cacti server, apart from including the `cacti` class, just needs to collect the devices now:

```
Cacti_device<<| tag == 'nyc-site' |>>
```

If one Cacti server handles all your machines, you can just omit the `tag` comparison:

```
Cacti_device<<| |>>
```

Once the module supports other Cacti resources, you can handle them in the same way. Let's look at an example from another popular monitoring solution.

Simplifying the configuration of Nagios

Puppet comes with support to manage the complete configuration of **Nagios** (and compatible versions of **Icinga**). Each configuration section can be represented by a distinct Puppet resource with types such as `nagios_host` or `nagios_service`.

There is an endeavour to remove this support from core Puppet. This does not mean that support will be discontinued, however. It will just move to yet another excellent Puppet module.

Each of your machines can export their individual `nagios_host` resources alongside their `host` and `cacti_device` resources. However, thanks to the diverse Nagios support, you can do even better.

Assuming that you have a module or class to wrap SSH handling (you are using a Forge module for the actual management, of course), you can handle monitoring from inside your own SSH server class. By adding the export to this class, you make sure that nodes that include the class (and only these nodes) will also get monitoring:

```
class site::ssh {
  # ...actual SSH management...
  @@nagios_service { "${::facts['networking']['fqdn']}-
  ssh":
  use        => 'ssh_template',
  host_name => $::facts['networking']['fqdn'],
  }
}
```

You probably know the drill by now, but let's repeat the mantra once more:

```
Nagios_service<<| |>>
```

With this collection, the Nagios host configures itself with all services that the agent manifests create.

For large Nagios configurations, you might want to consider reimplementing the Nagios types yourself, using simple defines that build the configuration from templates. The native types can be slower than the `file` resources in this case, because they have to parse the whole Nagios configuration on each run. The `file` resources can be much cheaper, as they rely on content-agnostic checksums.

Maintaining your central firewall

Speaking of useful features that are not part of the core of Puppet, you can manage the rules of your `iptables` firewall, of course. You need the `puppetlabs-firewall` module to make the appropriate types available. Then, each machine can (among other useful things) export its own required port forwarding to the firewall machines:

```
@@firewall { "150 forward port 443 to
${::facts['networking']['hostname']}":
    proto       => 'tcp',
    dport       => '443',
    destination => $public_ip_address,
    jump        => 'DNAT',
    todest      => $::facts['networking']['ipaddress'],
    tag         => 'segment03',
}
```

The `$public_ip_address` value is not a Facter fact, of course. Your node will have to be configured with the appropriate information. You can refer to Chapter 7, *New Features from Puppet 4 and 5*, for a good way to do this.

The title of a firewall rule resource conventionally begins with a three-digit index for ordering purposes. The firewall machines collect all these rules naturally:

```
Firewall<<| tag == 'segment03' |>>
```

As you can see, the possibilities for modeling distributed systems through exported Puppet resources are manifold. The simple pattern that we've iterated for several resource types suffices for a wide range of use cases. Combined with defined resource types, it allows you to flexibly enable your manifests to work together in order to form complex cluster setups with relatively little effort. The larger your clusters, the more work Puppet lifts from you through exports and collections.

Removing obsolete exports

When a node manifest stops exporting any resource, that resource's record is removed from PuppetDB once the node's catalog is compiled. This usually happens when the agent checks in with the master.

However, if you take an agent out of commission permanently, this will never happen. That's why you will need to remove those exports from the DB manually. Otherwise, other nodes will keep importing the old resources.

To clean such records from PuppetDB, use the `puppet node deactivate` command on the master server:

```
puppet node deactivate vax793.example.net
```

Setting defaults for resource parameters

Both exported and virtual resources are declared once, and are then collected in different contexts. The syntax is very similar, as are the concepts.

Sometimes, a central definition of a resource cannot be safely realized on all of your nodes, though; for example, consider the set of all your `user` resources. You will most likely wish to manage the user ID that is assigned to each account in order to make them consistent across your networks.

> This is often solved through LDAP or similar directories, but that is not possible for some sites.

Even if all accounts on almost all machines will be able to use their designated ID, there are likely to be some exceptions. On a few older machines, some IDs are probably being used for other purposes already, which cannot be changed easily. On such machines, creating users with these IDs will fail.

The accounts can be created if duplicate IDs are allowed, but that is not a solution to this problem duplicates are usually not desirable.

Fortunately, Puppet has a convenient way to express such exceptions. To give the nonstandard UID, 2066, to the user, felix, realize the resource with an attribute value specification:

```
User<| title == 'felix' |> {
  uid => '2066'
}
```

You can pass any property, parameter, or metaparameter that applies to the resource type in question. A value that you specify this way is final and cannot be overridden again.

This language feature is more powerful than the preceding example lets on. This is because the override is not limited to virtual and exported resources. You can override any resource from anywhere in your manifest. This allows for some remarkable constructs and shortcuts.

Consider, for example, the Cacti module that you created during the previous chapter. It declares a package resource in order to make sure that the software is installed. To that end, it specifies ensure => installed. If any user of your module needs Puppet to keep their packages up to date, this is not adequate though. The clean solution for this case is to add some parameters to the module's classes which allow the user to choose the ensure property value for the package and other resources. However, this is not really practical. Complex modules can manage hundreds of properties, and exposing them all through parameters would form a horribly confusing interface.

The override syntax can provide a simple and elegant workaround here. The manifest that achieves the desired result is very straightforward:

```
include cacti
Package<| title == 'cacti' |> { ensure => 'latest' }
```

For all its simplicity, this manifest will be hard to decipher for collaborators who are not familiar with the collector/override syntax. This is not the only problem with overrides. You cannot override the same attribute multiple times. This is actually a good thing, because any rules that resolve such conflicting overrides make it extremely difficult to predict the actual semantics of a manifest that contains multiple overrides of this kind.

Relying on this override syntax too much will make your manifests prone to conflicts. Combining the wrong classes will make the compiler stop creating the catalog. Even if you manage to avoid all conflicts, the manifests will become rather chaotic. It can be difficult to locate all active overrides for a given node. The resulting behavior of any class or define becomes hard to predict.

All things considered, it's safest to use overrides very sparingly.

The collectors are especially dangerous when used without a selector expression:

```
Package<| |> { before => Exec['send-software-list'] }
```

Not only will it realize all virtual resources of the given type. It will also force surprising attribute values on both virtual and regular resources of the same type.

Saving redundancy using resource defaults

The final language construct that this chapter introduces can save you quite some typing, or rather, it saves you from copying and pasting. Writing a long, repetitive manifest is not what costs you lots of time, of course. However, a briefer manifest is often more readable, and hence, more maintainable. You achieve this by defining resource defaults; attribute values that are used for resources that don't choose their own:

```
Mysql_grant {
   options    => ['GRANT'],
   privileges => ['ALL'],
   tables     => '*.*',
}
mysql_grant { 'root':
   ensure => 'present',
   user   => 'root@localhost',
}
mysql_grant { 'apache':
   ensure => 'present',
   user   => 'apache@10.0.1.%',
   tables => 'application.*',
}
mysql_grant { 'wordpress':
   ensure => 'present',
```

```
    user    => 'wordpress@10.0.5.1',
    tables  => 'wordpress.*',
  }
  mysql_grant { 'backup':
    ensure      => 'present',
    user        => 'backup@localhost',
    privileges  => [ 'SELECT', 'LOCK TABLE' ],
  }
```

By default, each grant should apply to all databases and comprise all privileges. This allows you to define each actual `mysql_grant` resource quite sparsely. Otherwise, you will have to specify the `privileges` property for all resources. The `options` attribute will be especially repetitive, because they are identical for all grants in this example.

Note that the ensure property is repetitive as well, but it was not included. It is considered good practice to exempt this attribute from resource defaults.

The `mysql_grant` resource type is not available in core Puppet. It's part of the `puppetlabs-mysql` module on the Forge.

Despite the convenience that this approach offers, it should not be used at each apparent opportunity. It has some downsides that you should keep in mind:

- The defaults can be surprising if they apply to resources that are declared at a lexical distance from the defaults' definition (such as several screens further down the manifest file)
- The defaults transcend the inclusion of classes and instantiation of defines

These two aspects form a dangerous combination. Defaults from a composite class can affect very distant parts of a manifest:

```
  class webserver {
    File { owner => 'www-data' }
    include apache, nginx, firewall, logging_client
    file {
      ...
    }
  }
```

Files declared in the `webserver` class should belong to a default user. However, this default takes effect recursively in the included classes as well. The `owner` attribute is a property: a resource that defines no value, for it just ignores its current state. A value that is specified in the manifest will be enforced by the agent. Often, you do not care about the owner of a managed file:

```
file { '/etc/motd': content => '...' }
```

However, because of the default `owner` attribute, Puppet will now mandate that this file belongs to `www-data`. To avoid this, you will have to unset the default by overwriting it with `undef`, which is Puppet's analog to the `nil` value:

```
File { owner => undef }
```

This can also be done in individual resources:

```
file { '/etc/motd': content => '...', owner => undef }
```

However, doing this constantly is hardly feasible. The latter option is especially unattractive, because it leads to more complexity in the manifest code, instead of simplifying it. After all, not defining a default `owner` attribute will be the cleaner way here.

The semantics that make defaults take effect in so many manifest areas is known as **dynamic scoping**. It used to apply to variable values as well and is generally considered harmful. One of the most decisive changes in Puppet 3.0 was the removal of dynamic variable scoping, in fact. Resource defaults still use it, but it is expected that this will change in a future release as well.

Resource defaults should be used with consideration and care. For some properties, such as `file mode`, `owner`, and `group`, they should usually be avoided.

Avoiding antipatterns

Speaking of things to avoid, there is a language feature that we will only address in order to advise great caution. Puppet comes with a function called `defined`, which allows you to query the compiler about resources that have been declared in the manifest:

```
if defined(File['/etc/motd']) {
  notify { 'This machine has a MotD': }
}
```

The problem with the concept is that it cannot ever be reliable. Even if the resource appears in the manifest, the compiler might encounter it later than the `if` condition. This is potentially very problematic, because some modules will try to make themselves portable through this construct:

```
if ! defined(Package['apache2']) {
  package { 'apache2':
    ensure => 'installed'
  }
}
```

The module author supposes that this resource definition will be skipped if the manifest declares `Package['apache2']` somewhere else. As explained, this method will only be effective if the block is evaluated late enough during the compiler run. The conflict can still occur if the compiler encounters the other declaration after this one.

The manifest's behavior becomes outright unpredictable if a manifest contains multiple occurrences of the same query:

```
class cacti {
  if !defined(Package['apache2']) {
    package { 'apache2': ensure => 'present' }
  }
}
class postfixadmin {
  if !defined(Package['apache2'] {
    package { 'apache2': ensure => 'latest' }
  }
}
```

The first block that is seen wins. This can even shift if unrelated parts of the manifest are restructured. You cannot predict whether a given manifest will use `ensure=>latest` for the `apache2` package or just use `installed`. The results become even more bizarre if such a block wants a resource removed through `ensure=>absent`, while the other does not.

The `defined` function has long been considered harmful, but there is no adequate alternative yet. The `ensure_resource` function from the `stdlib` module tries to make the scenario less problematic:

```
ensure_resource('package', 'apache2', { ensure => 'installed' })
```

By relying on this function instead of the preceding antipattern based around the `defined` function, you will avoid the unpredictable behavior of conflicting declarations. Instead, this will cause the compiler to fail when the declarations are passed to `ensure_resource`. This is still not a clean practice, though. Failed compilation is not a desirable alternative either.

Both functions should be avoided in favor of clean module structures with non-ambiguous resource declarations. More details on how to ensure reusable, composable, and stackable classes will be provided in `Chapter 9`, *Puppet Roles and Profiles*.

Summary

A template is a frequent occurrence and is one of the best ways for Puppet to manage dynamic file content. Evaluating each template requires extra effort from the compiler, but the gain in flexibility is usually worth it. Variables in templates have to be declared using the Puppet variable syntax with full namespace, or by prodding a hash with variable inside templates and classes.

The concept of virtual resources is much less ubiquitous. Virtual resources allow you to flexibly add certain entities to a node's catalog. The collector syntax that is used for this can also be used to override attribute values, which works for non-virtual resources as well.

Once PuppetDB is installed and configured, you can also export resources so that other node manifests can receive their configuration information. This allows you to model distributed systems quite elegantly.

The resource defaults are just a syntactic shortcut that help keep your manifest concise. They have to be used with care, though. Some language features, such as the `defined` function (and its module-based successor, which is the `ensure_resource` function), should be avoided if possible.

`Chapter 7`, *New Features from Puppet 4 and 5*, gives you an overview and introduction to the roles and profiles pattern, which is best practice for combining upstream modules with platform implementations.

7
New Features from Puppet 4 and 5

Now that we have a complete overview of the Puppet DSL and its concepts, it is time to look at the newest Puppet features, which were introduced with Puppet version 4. The parser, which compiles the catalog, was basically rewritten from scratch for better performance. The milestone release also added some missing functionality and coding principles.

Puppet 4 and newer versions do not only offer new functionality, but break with old practices and remove some functionality that is not considered best practice anymore. This necessitates that any existing manifest code needs proper testing, and potentially needs lots of changes to be compatible with Puppet 4.

Within this chapter, the following topics will be covered:

- Upgrading to Puppet 4
- Using the Puppet type system
- Learning lambdas and functions
- Creating Puppet 4 functions
- Leveraging the new template engine
- Handling multiline with HEREDOC
- Puppet 5 server metrics
- Breaking old practices

Upgrading to Puppet 4

Let's first look at how users of the older Puppet 3 series can approach the update.

Instead of upgrading your Puppet master machine, consider setting up a new server in parallel and migrating the service carefully. This has some advantages. For example, rolling back in case of problems is quite easy.

The new Puppet 4 and later versions can be installed in several ways:

- Using the Puppet Labs repositories, which will remove older Puppet packages
- This method means a hard cut without testing in advance, which is not recommended. The update to Puppet 4 and later versions should only take place after in-depth testing of your Puppet manifest code
- Installing as the Ruby gem extension or from tarball
- This approach requires a separate Ruby installation, which is not available on most modern Linux distributions. For Puppet 4, Ruby 2.1 is required. For Puppet 5, Ruby 2.4 is needed
- Update to Puppet 3.8, enable and migrate to the environment path settings, and enable the future parser only on a special testing environment
- The latter solution is the smartest and most backward compatible one

With Puppet 4 and later and the **All-in-One** (**AIO**) packaging from Puppet Labs, paths to Puppet configuration, modules, environments, and SSL certificates will change.

- Puppet 4 and 5 stores its configuration (`puppet.conf`) in `/etc/puppetlabs/puppet`
- Hiera config will be located in `/etc/puppetlabs/hiera/hiera.yaml`
- Puppet CA and certificates can be found at `/etc/puppetlabs/puppet/ssl`
- Puppet Code (environments and modules) are looked up in `/etc/puppetlabs/code/environments/`

Using Puppet 3.8 and environment directories

The new parser was introduced in Puppet 3.5 alongside the old parser. To make use of the new language features, a special configuration item needed to be set explicitly. This allowed early adopters and people interested in the new technology to test the parser and check for code incompatibilities in an early stage.

On Puppet 3.x, the new parser was subject to change without further notice. Therefore, it is recommended to upgrade to the latest 3.x release.

With directory environments, it is possible to specify environment specific settings within an `environment.conf` configuration file:

```
# /etc/puppet/environments/puppet_update/environment.conf
# environment config file for special puppet_update environment
parser = future
```

Next, all your Puppet code needs to be put into the newly created environment path, including node classification.

On each of the different node types, it is now possible to manually run:

```
puppet agent --test --environment=puppet_update --noop
```

Check both master and agent output and log files for any errors or unwanted changes and adapt your Puppet code if necessary.

The Puppet 4 and 5 master

 Make sure that your agents are prepared for operations with a Puppet 4 master. See the notes about agents in the following section.

Spinning up a new Puppet master is another approach. The following process assumes that the Puppet CA has been created using the DNS alt names setting in the `puppet.conf` file. If DNS alt names have been configured, it is required to completely recreate the Puppet CA.

Puppet CA needs to know about the **Common Name** (**CN**) of the Puppet master `fqdn`. It is possible to provide DNS alternative names, for which the CA will also be valid.

Normally, Puppet uses the master `fqdn` for the common name. But if you provide the configuration attribute `dns_alt_names` prior to generating the CA, this configuration option will be added to the CA.

It is highly recommended to configure `dns_alt_names`. Having this enabled allows you to scale up to multiple compile masters and add an additional Puppet master for the migration process.

To find out whether DNS alt names have been added, you can use the `puppet cert` command:

```
puppet cert list -all
```

This command will print all certificates. Check for the certificate of your Puppet master. For example, consider the following:

```
puppet cert list --all
+ "puppetmaster.example.net" (SHA256)
7D:11:33:00:94:B3:C4:48:D2:10:B3:C7:B0:38:71:28:C5:75:2C:61:3B:3E:63:C6:95:
7C:C9:DF:59:F7:C5:BE (alt names: "DNS:puppet", "DNS:puppet.example.net",
"DNS:puppetmaster.example.net")
```

The following steps will guide you through the Puppet 4 setup. On a Debian 7 based system, add the PC1 Puppet Labs repository:

```
curl -O http://apt.puppetlabs.com/puppetlabs-release-pc1-wheezy.deb
dpkg -i puppetlabs-release-pc1-wheezy.deb
apt-get update
apt-get install puppetserver puppet-agent
```

Do not start the Puppet server process yet! It is required to run the new Puppet 4 or 5 master as CA master, which needs the CA and certificates from the Puppet 3 master copied over to the new Puppet 4 master.

 As of this writing, the Puppet 5 Java-based master package requires Java 8 from backports for Debian 8. Besides this, PuppetDB 5 now needs PostgreSQL 9.6, whereas PuppetDB for Puppet 4 must be used along with PostgreSQL 9.4.

Within the next step, all Puppet agents need a change on the `puppet.conf` file. You will need to provide different settings for `ca_server` and `server`:

```
ini_setting { 'puppet_ca_server':
  path    => '/etc/puppet/puppet.conf',
  section => 'agent',
  setting => 'ca_server',
  value   => 'puppet4.example.net'
}
```

 The `ini_setting` resource type is available through the `puppetlabs-inifile` module from the Forge.

Now, place all your Puppet code on the new Puppet 4 master into an environment (`/etc/puppetlabs/code/environments/development/{manifests,modules}`).

Test your code for Puppet 4 errors by running the following command on each of your nodes:

```
puppet agent --test --noop --server puppet4.example.net --environment
development
```

Change your Puppet code to fix potential errors. Once no errors and no unwanted configuration changes occur on the Puppet 4 master and agents, your code is Puppet 4 compatible.

 Another approach to verify your Puppet code being fully functional on Puppet 4 and 5 is to compare catalogs. There are several solutions available. The most common ones are `puppetlabs-catalog_diff`, `zack-catalog`, and `octocatalog-diff`.

Updating the Puppet agent

It is important to make sure that your existing agents are prepared to operate with a master that is already at version 4. Check the following aspects:

- All agents should use the latest version of Puppet 3
- The agent configuration should specify `stringify_facts = false`

The latter step prepares you for the agent update, because Puppet 4 will always behave the same as that and refrain from converting all fact values to the string type.

Do make sure that you update to Puppet Server 2.1 or later. Passenger-based masters and Puppet Server 2.0 are not compatible with Puppet 3 agents.

> The Puppet online documentation contains many helpful details about this update path: `http://docs.puppetlabs.com/puppetserver/latest/compatibility_with_puppet_agent.html`.

Testing Puppet DSL code

Another approach for verifying whether the existing Puppet code will work on Puppet 4 is unit and integration testing using `rspec-puppet` and `beaker`. This procedure is not within the scope of this book.

Whether you started fresh with Puppet 4 or used one of the preceding procedures to migrate your Puppet 3 infrastructure, it is now time to discover the benefits of the new version.

Using the type system

Older Puppet versions supported a small set of data types only: `Bool`, `String`, `Array`, and `Hash`. The Puppet DSL had almost no functionality to check for consistent variable types. Consider the following scenario.

A parameterized class enables other users of your code base to change the behavior and output of the class:

```
class ssh (
  $server = true,
){
  if $server {
    include ssh::server
  }
}
```

This class definition checks whether the `server` parameter has been set to true. However, in this example, the class was not protected from wrong data usage:

```
class { 'ssh':
  server => 'false',
}
```

In this class declaration, the server parameter has been given a string instead of a bool value. Since the `false` string is not empty, the if `$server` condition actually passes. This is not what the user will expect.

Within Puppet 3, it was recommended to add parameter validation using several functions from the `stdlib` module:

```
class ssh (
  $server = true,
){
  validate_bool($server)
  if $server {
    include ssh::server
  }
}
```

With one parameter only, this seems to be a good way. But what if you have many parameters? How do we deal with complex data types as hashes?

This is where the type system comes into play. The type system knows about many generic data types and follows patterns that are also used in many other modern programming languages.

Puppet differentiates between core data types and abstract data types. Core data types are the real data types, the ones which are mostly used in Puppet Code:

- String
- Integer, float, and numeric
- Boolean
- Array
- Hash
- Regexp
- Undef
- Default

In the given example, the `server` parameter should be checked to always contain a bool value. The code can be simplified to the following pattern:

```
class ssh (
  Boolean $server = true,
){
  if $server {
    include ssh::server
  }
}
```

If the parameter is not given a Boolean value, Puppet will throw an error, explaining which parameter has a non-matching data type:

```
class { 'ssh':
  server = 'false',
}
```

The error displayed is as follows:

```
root@puppetmaster# puppet apply ssh.pp
Error: Expected parameter 'server' of 'Class[Ssh]' to have type Boolean,
got String at ssh.pp:2 on node puppetmaster.example.net
```

The `Numeric`, `Float`, and `Integer` data types have some more interesting aspects when it comes to variables and their type.

Puppet will automatically recognize `Integers`, consisting of numbers (either with or without the minus sign) and not having a decimal point.

`Floats` are recognized by the decimal point. When doing arithmetic algebra on a combination of an `Integer` and a `Float`, the result will always be a `Float`.

`Floats` between -1 and 1 must be written with a leading 0 digit prior to the decimal point; otherwise, Puppet will throw an error.

Besides this, Puppet has support for the decimal, octal, and hexadecimal notation, as known from C-like languages:

- A nonzero decimal must not start with a 0
- Octal values must start with a leading 0
- Hexadecimal values have `0x` as the prefix

Puppet will automatically convert numbers into strings during the interpolation: (`"Value of number: ${number}"`).

 Puppet will not convert strings to numbers. To make this happen, you can simply add 0 to a string to convert:

```
$ssh_port = '22'
$ssh_port_integer = 0 + $ssh_port
```

The `Default` data type is a little special. It does not directly refer to a data type, but can be used in selectors and case statements:

```
$enable_real = $enable ? {
  Boolean => $enable,
  String  => str2bool($enable),
  default => fail('Unsupported value for ensure. Expected either
   bool or string.'),
}
```

Abstract data types are constructs that are useful for a more sophisticated or permissive Type checking:

- Scalar
- Collection
- Variant
- Data
- Pattern
- Enum
- Tuple
- Struct
- Optional
- Catalog entry
- Type
- Any
- Callable

Assume that a parameter will only accept strings from a limited set. Only checking for being of type `String` is not sufficient. In this scenario, the `Enum` type is useful; a list of valid values are specified for it:

```
class ssh (
  Boolean $server = true,
  Enum['des','3des','blowfish'] $cipher = 'des',
){
  if $server {
    include ssh::server
  }
}
```

If the listen parameter is not set to one of the listed elements, Puppet will throw an error:

```
class { 'ssh':
  ciper => 'foo',
}
```

The following error is displayed:

```
puppet apply ssh.pp
Error: Expected parameter 'ciper' of 'Class[Ssh]' to have type
Enum['des','3des','blowfish'] got String at ssh.pp:2 on node
puppetmaster.example.net
```

Sometimes, it is difficult to use specific data types, because the parameter might be set to an `undef` value. Think of a `userlist` parameter that might be empty (`undef`) or set to an arbitrary array of strings.

This is what the `Optional` type is for:

```
class ssh (
  Boolean $server = true,
  Enum['des','3des','blowfish'] $cipher = 'des',
  Optional[Array[String]] $allowed_users = undef,
){
  if $server {
    include ssh::server
  }
}
```

Again, using a wrong data type will lead to a Puppet error:

```
class { 'ssh':
  allowed_users => 'foo',
}
```

The error displayed is as follows:

```
puppet apply ssh.pp
Error: Expected parameter 'userlist' of 'Class[Ssh]' to have type
Optional[Array[String]], got String at ssh.pp:2 on node
puppetmaster.example.net
```

In the previous example, we used a data type composition. This means that data types can have more information for type checking.

Let's assume that we want to set the ssh service port in our class. Normally, ssh should run on a privileged port between 1 and 1023. In this case, we can restrict the integer data type to only allow numbers between 1 and 1023 by passing additional information:

```
class ssh (
  Boolean $server = true,
  Optional[Array[String]] $allowed_users = undef,
  Integer[1,1023] $sshd_port,
){
  if $server {
    include ssh::server
  }
}
```

As always, providing a wrong parameter will lead to an error:

```
class { 'ssh':
  sshd_port => 'ssh',
}
```

The preceding line of code gives the following error:

```
puppet apply ssh.pp
Error: Expected parameter 'sshd_port' of 'Class[Ssh]' to have type
Integer[1, 1023], got String at ssh.pp:2 on node puppetmaster.example.net
```

Complex hashes that use multiple data types that are very complicated to describe using the new type system.

When using the Hash type, it is only possible to check for a hash in general, or for a hash with keys of a specific type. You can optionally verify the minimum and maximum number of elements in the hash.

The following example provides a working hash type check:

```
$hash_map = {
  'ben'       => {
    'uid'     => 2203,
    'home'    => '/home/ben',
  },
  'jones'     => {
    'uid'     => 2204,
    'home'    => 'home/jones',
  }
}
```

Notably, the home entry for user jones is missing the leading slash:

```
class users (
  Hash $users
){
  notify { 'Valid Hash': }
}
class { 'users':
  users => $hash_map,
}
```

Running the preceding code, gives us the following output:

```
puppet apply hash.pp
Notice: Compiled catalog for puppetmaster.example.net in environment
production in 0.32 seconds
Notice: Valid hash
Notice: /Stage[main]/Users/Notify[Valid hash]/message: defined 'message' as
'Valid hash'
Notice: Applied catalog in 0.03 seconds
```

With the preceding notation, the data type is valid. Yet there are errors inside the hash map.

Checking content of Arrays or Hashes requires the use of another abstract data type: Tuple (used for Arrays) or Struct (used for Hashes).

However, the Struct data type will work only when the key names are from a known limited set, which is not the case in the given example.

In this special case, we have two possibilities:

- Extend the hash data type to know about the hash internal structure
- Wrap the type data into a define, which makes use of all keys using the key function (from stdlib)

The first solution is as follows:

```
class users (
  Hash[
    String,
    Struct[ { 'uid' => Integer,
              'home' => Pattern[ /^\/.*/ ] } ]
  ] $users
){
  notify { 'Valid hash': }
}
```

However, the error message is hard to understand when the data types are not matching:

```
puppet apply hash.pp
Error: Expected parameter 'users' of 'Class[Users]' to have type
Hash[String, Struct[{'uid'=>Integer, 'home'=>Pattern[/^\/.*/]}]], got
Struct[{'ben'=>Struct[{'uid'=>Integer, 'home'=>String}],
'jones'=>Struct[{'uid'=>Integer, 'home'=>String}]}] at hash.pp:32 on node
puppetmaster.example.net
```

The second solution gives a smarter hint on which data might be wrong:

```
define users::user (
  Integer         $uid,
  Pattern[/^\/.*/] $home,
){
  notify { "User: ${title}, UID: ${uid}, HOME: ${home}": }
}
```

This defined type is then employed from within the users class:

```
class users (
  Hash[String, Hash] $users
){
  $keys = keys($users)
  each($keys) |String $username| {
    users::user{ $username:
      uid  => $users[$username]['uid'],
      home => $users[$username]['home'],
    }
  }
}
```

With the wrong submitted data in the hash, you will receive the following
error message:

```
puppet apply hash.pp
Error: Expected parameter 'home' of 'Users::User[jones]' to have type
Pattern[/^\/.*/], got String at hash.pp:23 on node puppetmaster.example.net
```

The error message is pointing to the home parameter of the user jones, which is given in
the hash. The correct hash is as follows:

```
$hash_map = {
  'ben'    => {
    'uid'  => 2203,
    'home' => '/home/ben',
  },
  'jones'  => {
    'uid'  => 2204,
    'home' => '/home/jones',
  }
}
```

The preceding code produces the expected result as follows:

```
puppet apply hash.pp
Notice: Compiled catalog for puppetmaster.example.net in environment
production in 0.33 seconds
Notice: User: ben, UID: 2203, HOME: /home/ben
Notice: /Stage[main]/Users/Users::User[ben]/Notify[User: ben, UID: 2203,
HOME: /home/ben]/message: defined 'message' as 'User: ben, UID: 2203, HOME:
/home/ben'
Notice: User: jones, UID: 2204, HOME: /home/jones
Notice: /Stage[main]/Users/Users::User[jones]/Notify[User: jones, UID:
2204, HOME: /home/jones]/message: defined 'message' as 'User: jones, UID:
2204, HOME: /home/jones'
Notice: Applied catalog in 0.03 seconds
```

Next to the existing data types, Puppet offers the possibility to also build data types based
on existing ones.

Within the last example we were matching a regular expression to identify an absolute
path, but sometimes regular expressions might become very complex and hard to
understand. This is where the type declaration comes into place.

A type declaration must be part of a module, use the module namespace as a prefix, and must be placed into the types directory.

```
# stlib/types/absolutepath.pp
type Stdlib::Absolutepath = Variant[Stdlib::Windowspath, Stdlib::Unixpath]
```

The Windows and Unix path types have proper regular expressions.

The type system becomes handy when you want to validate a very specific data type. Think about a firewall module where you want to check for IPv4 or IPv6 addresses.

We can use the same pattern same as the `absolutepath` data type:

```
#firewall/types/ipaddress.pp
type Firewall::Ipaddress = Variant[Firewall::Ipv4, Firewall::Ipv6]
```

The preceding manifest uses the `each` function, another part of the Puppet 4 language. The next section explores it in greater detail.

Learning lambdas and functions

Functions have long been an essential part of Puppet. Due to the new type system, a complete new set of functions have become possible functions with different behavior based on parameter data types.

To understand functions, we first have to take a look at lambdas, which are introduced in Puppet 4. Lambdas represent a snippet of Puppet code, which can be used in functions. Syntactically, lambdas consist of an optional type and at least one variable with optional defaults set, enclosed in pipe signs (|), followed by Puppet code inside a block of curly braces:

```
$packages = ['htop', 'less', 'vim']
each($packages) |String $package|
{
     package { $package:
       ensure => latest,
   }
}
```

Lambdas are typically used on functions. The preceding example uses the `each` function on the `$packages` variable, iterating over its contents, setting the lambda variable `$package` within each iteration to the values `htop`, `less`, and `vim`, respectively. The Puppet code block uses the lambda variable inside a resource type declaration afterwards.

 The Puppet code in curly braces has to ensure that no duplicate resource declaration occurs.

Since Puppet now knows about data types, you can interact and work with variables, and the data inside, in a far more elegant way.

in functions for arrays and hashes:

- Puppet 4 comes with a whole set of built-in functions for arrays and hashes: each
- slice
- filter
- map
- reduce
- with

We have already seen the `each` function in action. Prior to Puppet 4, one needed to wrap the desired Puppet resource types into `define` and declare the `define` type using an array:

```
class puppet_symlinks {
  $symlinks = [ puppet', 'facter', 'hiera' ]
  puppet_symlinks::symlinks { $symlinks: }
}

define puppet_symlinks::symlinks {
  file { "/usr/local/bin/${title}":
    ensure => link,
    target => "/opt/puppetlabs/bin/${title}",
  }
}
```

With this concept, the action (create the `symlink`) was put into a define type and was no longer directly visible in the manifest. The new iteration approach keeps the action in the same location:

```
class puppet_symlinks {
  $symlinks = [ 'puppet', 'facter', 'hiera' ]
  $symlinks.each | String $symlink | {
```

```
  file { "/usr/local/bin/${symlink}":
    ensure => link,
    target => "/opt/puppetlabs/bin/${symlink}",
  }
 }
}
```

Did you recognize that, this time, we used another approach of using a function? In the first example, we used the Puppet 3 style function calls:

```
function($variable)
```

Puppet 4 also supports the postfix notation, where the function is appended to its parameter using a dot:

```
$variable.function
```

Puppet 4 supports both ways of using a function. This allows you to keep adhering to your code style and make use of the new functionality.

Let's run though the other functions for arrays and hashes:

- The `slice` function allows you to split up and group an array or a hash. It needs an additional parameter (integer), defining how many objects should be grouped together:

  ```
  $array = [ '1', '2', '3', '4']
  $array.slice(2) |$slice| {
    notify { "Slice: ${slice}": }
  }
  ```

- This code will produce the following output:

  Notice: Slice: [1, 2]
  Notice: Slice: [3, 4]

- When using the slice functions on a hash, one receives the keys (according to the amount of grouped keys) and accordingly, the sub hash:

  ```
  $hash = {
    'key 1' => {'value11' => '11', 'value12' => '12',},
    'key 2' => {'value21' => '21', 'value22' => '22',},
    'key 3' => {'value31' => '31', 'value32' => '32',},
    'key 4' => {'value41' => '41', 'value42' => '42',},
  }
  ```

```
$hash.slice(2) |$hslice| {
  notify { "HSlice: ${hslice}": }
}
```

- This will return the following output:

```
Notice: HSlice: [[key1, {value11 => 11, value12 =>
12}],
[key2, {value21 => 21, value22 => 22}]]
Notice: HSlice: [[key3, {value31 => 31, value32 =>
32}],
[key4, {value41 => 41, value42 => 42}]]
```

- The `filter` function can be used to filter out specific entries inside an array or hash.

- When used on an array, all elements are passed to the code block and the code block evaluates whether the entry does match. This is very useful if you want to filter out items of an array (for example, packages which should be installed):

```
$pkg_array = [ 'libjson', 'libjson-devel', 'libfoo', 'libfoo-devel'
]
$dev_packages = $pkg_array.filter |$element| {
  $element =~ /devel/
}
notify { "Packages to install: ${dev_packages}": }
```

- This will return the following output:

```
Notice: Packages to install: [libjson-devel, libfoo-
devel]
```

- The behavior on hashes is different. When using hashes, one has to provide two lambda variables: `key` and `value`. You might want to only add users that have a specific `gid` set:

```
$hash = {
  'jones' => {
    'gid' => 'admin',
  },
  'james' => {
    'gid' => 'devel',
  },
  'john'  => {
    'gid' => 'admin',
  },
}
```

```
$user_hash = $hash.filter |$key, $value| {
  $value['gid'] =~ /admin/
}
$user_list = keys($user_hash)
notify { "Users to create: ${user_list}": }
```

- This will return only the users from the admin gid:

Notice: Users to create: [jones, john]

Creating Puppet 4 functions

The Puppet 3 functions API has some limitations and is missing features. The new function API in Puppet 4 improves upon that substantially.

Some of the limitations of the old functions are as follows:

- The functions had no automatic type checking
- These functions had to have a unique name due to a flat namespace
- These functions were not private and, hence, could be used anywhere
- The documentation could not be retrieved without running the Ruby code

Running on Puppet 3 requires functions to be in a module in the lib/puppet/parser/functions directory. Therefore, people referred to these functions as **parser functions**, but this name is misleading. Functions are unrelated to the Puppet parser.

In Puppet 4, functions have to be put into a module in path lib/puppet/functions.

This is how you create a function that will return the hostname of the Puppet master:

```
# modules/utils/lib/puppet/functions/resolver.rb
require 'socket'
Puppet::Functions.create_function(:resolver) do
  def resolver()
    Socket.gethostname
  end
end
```

Using dispatch adds type checking for attributes. Depending on desired functionality, one might have multiple dispatch blocks (checking for different data types). Each dispatch can refer to another defined Ruby method inside the function. This reference is possible by using the same names for dispatch and the Ruby method.

The following example code should get additional functionality; depending on the type of argument, the function should either return the hostname of the local system, or use DNS to get the hostname from an IPv4 address or the `ipaddress` for a given hostname:

```
require 'resolv'
require 'socket'
Puppet::Functions.create_function(:resolver) do
  dispatch :ip_param do
    param 'Pattern[/^(?:[0-9]{1,3}\.){3}[0-9]{1,3}$/]', :ip
  end
  dispatch :fqdn_param do
    param 'Pattern[/^([a-z0-9\.].*$/]', :fqdn
  end
  dispatch :no_param do
  end

  def no_param
    Socket.gethostname
  end
  def ip_param(ip)
    Resolv.getname(ip)
  end
  def fqdn_param(fqdn)
    Resolv.getaddress(fqdn)
  end
end
```

At the beginning of the file, we have to load some Ruby modules to allow the DNS name resolution and to find the local hostname.

The first two `dispatch` sections check for the data type of the parameter value and set a unique symbol. The last `dispatch` section does not check for data types, which matches when no parameter was given.

Each defined Ruby method uses the name of the according `dispatch` and executes Ruby code depending on the parameter type.

Now, the resolver function can be used from inside the Puppet manifest code in three different ways:

```
class resolver {
  $localname = resolver()
  notify { "Without argument resolver returns local
  hostname:
  ${localname}": }

  $remotename = resolver('puppetlabs.com')
```

```
notify { "With argument puppetlabs.com: ${remotename}":
}

$remoteip = resolver('8.8.8.8')
notify { "With argument 8.8.8.8: ${remoteip}": }
}
```

When declaring this class, the following output will show up:

```
puppet apply -e 'include resolver'
Notice: Compiled catalog for puppetmaster.example.net in environment
production in 0.35 seconds
...
Notice: Without argument resolver returns local hostname: puppetmaster
Notice: With argument puppetlabs.com: 52.10.10.141
Notice: With argument 8.8.8.8: google-public-dns-a.google.com
Notice: Applied catalog in 0.04 seconds
```

With Puppet 3 functions, it was impossible to have two functions of the same name. One always had to check whether duplicate functions appeared when making use of a new module.

The Puppet 4 functions now offer the possibility of using namespacing just the same as classes.

Let's migrate our function into the class namespace:

```
# modules/utils/lib/puppet/functions/resolver/resolve.rb
require 'resolv'
require 'socket'
Puppet::Functions.create_function(:'resolver::resolve') do
  # the rest of the function is identical to the example given
    # above
end
```

In the example, the code needs to be in
`resolver/lib/puppet/functions/resolver/resolve.rb`, which corresponds to
`function name: 'resolver::resolve'`.

Functions with namespaces are invoked as usual:

```
class resolver {
  $localname = resolver::resolve()
  $remotename = resolver::resolve('puppetlabs.com')
  $remoteip = resolver::resolve('8.8.8.8')
}
```

Leveraging the new template engine

In Chapter 6, *The Puppet Beginners Advanced Parts*, we introduced templates and the ERB template engine. In Puppet 4, an alternative was added: the EPP template engine. The major differences between the template engines are as follows:

- In ERB templates, you cannot specify a variable in Puppet syntax (`$variable_name`)
- ERB templates will not accept parameters
- In EPP templates, you will use the Puppet DSL syntax instead of Ruby syntax

The EPP template engine requires scoped variables from modules:

```
# motd file - managed by Puppet
This system is running on <%= $::operatingsystem %>
```

The manifest defines the following local variable: `<%= $motd::local_variable %>`. The EPP templates also have a unique extension: they can take typed parameters.
To make use of this, a template has to start with a parameter declaration block:

```
<%- | String $local_variable,
      Array  $local_array
| -%>
```

These parameters are not as variables from Puppet manifests. Instead, one must pass parameters using the `epp` function:

```
epp('template/test.epp', {'local_variable' => 'value', 'local_array' =>
['value1', 'value2'] })
```

A template without parameters should only be used when the template is used exclusively by one module, so that it is safe to rely on the availability of Puppet variables to customize the content.

Using the EPP template function with parameters is recommended when a template is used from several places. By declaring the parameters at the beginning, it is especially clear what data the template requires.

There is a specific difference between the template engines when iterating over arrays and hashes. The ERB syntax uses Ruby code with unscoped, local variables, whereas the EPP syntax requires specifying Puppet DSL code:

```
# ERB syntax
<% @array.each do |element| -%>
<%= element %>
```

```
<% end -%>

# EPP syntax
<% $array.each |$element| { -%>
<%= $element %>
<% } -%>
```

The inline ERB function was also supplemented with inline EPP. Using the inline EPP, one can specify a small snippet of EPP code to get evaluated:

```
file {'/etc/motd':
  ensure  => file,
  content => inline_epp("Welcome to <%= $::fqdn %>\n")
}
```

Prior to Puppet 4, it was inconvenient to pass more than a small code snippet. With Puppet 4 and the HEREDOC support, complex templates in combination with `inline_epp` are easier and better readable.

Handling multiline with HEREDOC

Writing multiline file fragments in Puppet mostly resulted in code that was hard to read, mostly due to indentation. With Puppet 4, the `heredoc` style was added. It is now possible to specify a `heredoc` tag and marker:

```
$motd_content = @(EOF)
  This system is managed by Puppet
  local changes will be overwritten by next Puppet run.
EOF
```

The `heredoc` tag starts with an @ sign followed by arbitrary string enclosed in parenthesis. The `heredoc` marker is the string given in the tag.

If variables are required inside the `heredoc` document, the variable interpolation can be enabled by putting the tag string in double quotes. Variables inside the `heredoc` are written the same as Puppet DSL variables: a dollar sign followed by the scope and the variable name:

```
$motd_content = @("EOF")
  Welcome to ${::fqdn}.
  This system is managed by Puppet version ${::puppetversion}.
  Local changes will be overwritten by the next Puppet run
EOF
```

Normally, `heredoc` does not handle escape sequences. Escape sequences need to be enabled explicitly. As of Puppet 4.2, `heredoc` has the following escape sequences available:

- * \n Newline
- * \r Carriage return
- * \t Tab
- * \s Space
- * \\$ Literal dollar sign (preventing interpolation)
- * \u Unicode character
- \L Nothing (ignore line breaks in source code)

Enabled escape sequences have to be placed behind the string of the `heredoc` tag:

```
$modt_content = @("EOF"/tn)
Welcome to ${::fqdn}.\n\tThis system is managed by Puppet version
${::puppetversion}.\n\tLocal changes will be overwritten on next Puppet
run.
EOF
```

In the example, the text always starts in the first column, which makes it hard to read and stands out from the code around it, which will usually be indented by some amount of whitespace.

It is possible to strip indentation by placing whitespaces and a pipe sign in front of the `heredoc` marker. The pipe sign will indicate the first character of each line:

```
$motd_content = @("EOF")
    Welcome to ${::fqdn}.
    This system is managed by Puppet version ${::puppetversion}.
    Local changes will be overwritten on next Puppet run.
    | EOF
```

Now `heredoc` and `inline_epp` can be easily combined:

```
class my_motd (
  Optional[String] $additional_content = undef
){
  $motd_content = @(EOF)
    Welcome to <%= $::fqdn %>.
    This system is managed by Puppet version
    <%= $::puppetversion %>.
    Local changes will be overwritten on next Puppet run.
    <% if $additional_content != undef { -%>
    <%= $additional_content %>
    <% } -%>
```

```
  | EOF
file { '/etc/motd':
  ensure  => file,
  content => inline_epp($motd_content, {
  additional_content => $additional_content } ),
}
}
```

Declaring this class will give the following result in the motd file:

```
puppet apply -e 'include my_motd'
Welcome to puppetmaster.example.net.
This system is managed by Puppet version 4.2.1.
Local changes will be overwritten on next Puppet run.
```

> When using heredoc in combination with inline_epp, you want to take care to not quote the heredoc start tag. Otherwise, the variable substitution will take place prior to the inline_epp function call.

Using Puppet 5 server metrics

With Puppetserver Version 5 the former Puppet Enterprise only metrics system has been ported to Puppet Open Source.

The metrics system allows you to read internal information like compile times, status of file serving and function runtimes from a JMX console or to push the data to a graphite system.

Enabling the metrics system is straightforward by editing the puppet server metrics.conf file located at /etc/puppetlabs/puppetserver/conf.d/metrics.conf.

There are three important settings. At the metrics.server-id one can specify an ID which is later used in the Grafana dashboard. The metrics.registry.puppetserver.reporters.graphite.enabled value must be set to true and the metrics.reporters.graphite hash must mention the graphite hostname and port and the update interval setting:

```
# settings related to metrics
metrics: {
  # a server id that will be used as part of the namespace
  for metrics produced
  # by this server
  server-id: "puppet.bi.example42.com"
  registries: {
```

```
    puppetserver: {
      # specify metrics to allow in addition to those in
      the default list
      #metrics-allowed: ["compiler.compile.production"]
      # enable or disable JMX metrics reporter
      jmx: {
        enabled: true
      }
      # enable or disable Graphite metrics reporter
      graphite: {
        enabled: true
      }
    }
  }
  # this section is used to configure settings for
  reporters that will send
  # the metrics to various destinations for external
  viewing
  reporters: {
    graphite: {
      host: "10.0.4.2"
      port: "2003"
      update-interval-seconds: 5
    }
  }
  metrics-webservice: {
    jolokia: {
      # Enable or disable the Jolokia-based metrics/v2
      endpoint.
      # Default is true.
      # enabled: false
      # Configure any of the settings listed at:
      #
      https://jolokia.org/reference/html/agents.html#war-
      agent-installation
      servlet-init-params: {
        # Specify a custom security policy:
        # https://jolokia.org/reference/html/security.html
        # policyLocation:
        "file:///etc/puppetlabs/puppetserver/jolokia-
        access.xml"
      }
    }
  }
}
```

Don't forget to restart the puppetserver process after doing changes.

For automated setup one wants to use the puppetlabs-hocon module which is able to set all desired values:

```
Hocon_setting {
  path    =>
  '/etc/puppetlabs/puppetserver/conf.d/metrics.conf',
  notify => Service['puppetserver'],
  }
  hocon_setting {'server metrics server-id':
    ensure  => present,
    setting => 'metrics.server-id',
    value   => 'localhost',
  }
  hocon_setting {'server metrics reporters graphite':
    ensure  => present,
    setting =>
  'metrics.registries.puppetserver.reporters.graphite.enabled',
    value   => true,
  }
  hocon_setting {'server metrics graphite host':
    ensure  => present,
    setting => 'metrics.reporters.graphite.host',
    value   => $graphite_server,
  }
  hocon_setting {'server metrics graphite port':
    ensure  => present,
    setting => 'metrics.reporters.graphite.port',
    value   => 2003,
  }
  hocon_setting {'server metrics graphite update
  interval':
    ensure  => present,
    setting => 'metrics.reporters.graphite.update-
    interval-seconds',
    value   => 5,
  }
```

The setup of praphite is beyond the scope of this book. There is a puppet module available for evaluation purpose (http://github.com/tuxmea/puppet-grafanadash).

This module installs and configures elasticsearch, graphite, and grafana on a CentOS 7 system.

You only need to include the `grfanadash::dev` class on a node:

```
node 'graphite.example.com' {    include grafanadash::dev }
```

Afterwards you can access graphite on `http://graphite.example.com` and grafana at `http://graphite.example-com:10000`. Within the grafana dashboard one can load the `.json` file from module examples folder.

Please be aware that it might take up to 10 minutes prior values will show up in grafana.

Breaking old practices

When Puppet Labs decided to work on the parser and on the new features, they also decided to remove some features that had already been deprecated for a couple of releases.

Converting node inheritance

Node inheritance has been considered good practice during older Puppet releases. To avoid too much code on the node level, a generic, nonexistent host was created (`basenode`) and the real nodes inherited from `basenode`:

```
node basenode {
  include security
  include ldap
  include base
}
node 'www01.example.net' inherits 'basenode' {
  class { 'apache': }
  include apache::mod::php
  include webapplication
}
```

This node classification is no longer supported by Puppet 4.

As of 2012, the roles and profiles pattern became increasingly popular, bringing new methods on how to allow smart node classification. From a technical point of view, roles and profiles are Puppet classes. The profile module wraps technical modules and adapts their usage to the existing infrastructure by providing data such as `ntp` servers and `ssh` configuration options. The role module describes system business use cases and makes use of the declared profiles:

```
class profile::base {
  include security
  include ldap
  include base
}
class profile::webserver {
  class { 'apache': }
  include apache_mod_php
}

class role::webapplication {
  include profile::base
  include profile::webserver
  include profile::webapplication
}

node 'www01.example.net' {
  include role::webapplication
}
```

The final chapter will describe the roles and profiles pattern in some more detail.

Dealing with bool algebra on Strings

A minor change with a huge impact is the change of empty string comparison. Prior to Puppet 4, one could test for either an unset variable or a variable containing an empty string by checking for the variable:

```
class ssh (
  $server = true,
){
```

```
    if $server {...}
}
```

The `ssh` class behaved similarly ($server evaluates to true) when used within the following different declarations:

```
include ssh
class { 'ssh': server => 'yes', }
```

Disabling the server section in the `ssh` class could be achieved by the following class declarations:

```
class { 'ssh': server => false, }
class { 'ssh': server => '', }
```

The behavior of the last example (empty string) changed in Puppet 4. The empty string now equals a true value in Boolean context, just as in Ruby. If your code makes use of this way of variable checking, you need to add the check for empty string to retain the same behavior with Puppet 4:

```
class ssh (
   $server = true,
){
   if $server and $server != '' {...}
}
```

Using strict variable naming

Variables sometimes look the same as constants and exhibit the following features:

- Variables cannot be declared again
- In the scope of one node, most variables are static (`hostname`, `fqdn`, and so on)

Sometimes, developers prefer to write the variables in capital letters due to the previously mentioned items, to make them look the same as Ruby constants.

With Puppet 4, variable names must not start with a capital letter:

```
class variables
{
   $Local_var = 'capital variable'
   notify { "Local capital var: ${Local_var}": }
}
```

Declaring this class will now produce the following error message:

```
root@puppetmaster:/etc/puppetlabs/code/environments/production/modules#
puppet apply -e 'include variables'
Error: Illegal variable name, The given name 'Local_var' does not conform
to the naming rule /^((::)?[a-z]\w*)*((::)?[a-z_]\w*)$/ at
/etc/puppetlabs/code/environments/production/modules/variables/manifests/in
it.pp:3:3 on node puppetmaster.example.net
```

Learning the new reference syntax

Due to the type system and due to the reason that Puppet 4 now takes everything as an expression, one has to name references on other declared resources properly. References now have some strict regulations:

- No whitespace between reference type and opening bracket
- The reference title (used without quotes) must not be spelled with a capital letter

The following will produce errors on Puppet 4:

```
User [Root]
User[Root]
```

Starting with Puppet 4, references have to be written in the following pattern:

```
Type['title']
```

Our example needs to be changed to:

```
User['root']
```

Cleaning hyphens in names

Many modules (even on the module Forge) have used the hyphen in the module name. The hyphen is now no longer a string character, but a mathematical operator (subtraction). In consequence, hyphens are now strictly forbidden in the following descriptors:

- The module name
- Any class name
- Names of defined types

When using modules with hyphens, the hyphen needs to be removed or replaced with a string character (for example, the underscore).

This is possible with older versions, as follows:

```
class syslog-ng {...}

include syslog-ng
```

Now, the new style is as follows:

```
class syslog_ng {
  ...
}

include syslog_ng
```

No Ruby DSL anymore

Some people used the possibility to put .rb files as manifests inside modules. These .rb files contained Ruby code and were mostly needed for working with data. Puppet 4 now has data types that make this obsolete.

The support for these Ruby manifests has been removed in Puppet 4.

Relative class name resolution

With Puppet 3 and older, it was required to specify absolute class names in case that a local class name was identical to another module:

```
# in module "mysql"
class mysql {
  ...
}
# in module "application"
class application::mysql {
  include mysql
}
```

Within the scope of the `application::` namespace, Puppet 3 would search this namespace for a `mysql` class to be included. Effectively, the `application::mysql` class would include itself. However, this was not what we intended to do. We were looking for the `mysql` module instead. As a workaround, everybody was encouraged to specify the absolute path to the `mysql` module class:

```
class application::mysql {
   include ::mysql
}
```

This relative name resolution no longer applies in Puppet 4. The original example works now.

Dealing with different data types

Because Puppet 3 was not aware of the different data types
(mostly everything was dealt with as being of type string), it was possible to combine several different data types.

Puppet 4 is now very strict when it comes to combining different data types. The easiest example is dealing with float and integer; when adding a float and an integer, the result will be of type float.

Combining actions on different data types, such as string and bool, will now result in an error. The following code will work:

```
case $::operatingsystemmajrelease {
  '8': {
    include base::debian::jessie
  }
}
```

On the other hand, the following code will not work:

```
if $::operatingsystemmajrelease > 7 {
  include base::debian::jessie
}
```

You will receive the following error message:

```
Error: Evaluation Error: Comparison of: String > Integer, is not possible.
Caused by 'A String is not comparable to a non String'
```

Review the comparison of different Facter variables carefully. Some Facter variables, such as `operatingsystemmajrelease`, return data of the type string; whereas `processorcount` returns an integer value.

Summary

Upgrading to Puppet 3 should be done in a step-by-step procedure where your existing code will be evaluated using Puppet 3.8 and the new parser.

Thanks to the type system, it is now possible to deal with data in a far more elegant way directly in your Puppet DSL code. The new functions API allows you to immediately recognize to which module a function belongs by using namespaces. Similar functions can now be combined within a single file by making use of the `dispatch` method and data types, allowing a form of function overloading.

The new EPP templates offer better understanding of variable sources by using the Puppet syntax for variable references. Passing parameters to templates will allow you to make use of modules in a more flexible way.

Combining EPP templates and the HEREDOC syntax will allow you to keep template code and data directly visible inside your classes.

In the upcoming chapter, you will learn about Hiera and how it can help you bring order to a scalable Puppet code base.

8

Separation of Code and Data with Hiera

Working through the first seven chapters, you have used the basic structural elements of Puppet in numerous examples and contexts. There has been a quick demonstration of the more advanced language features, and you should have a good idea of what distinguishes the manifest writing process in Puppet 4 from those of the earlier releases.

For all their expressive power, manifests do have some limitations. A manifest that is designed by the principles taught up to this point mixes logic with data. Logic is not only evident in control structures, such as `if` and `else`, but it also emerges from the network of classes and defines that include and instantiate one another.

However, you cannot configure a machine by just including some generic classes. Many properties of a given system are individual and must be passed as parameters. This can have maintenance implications for a manifest that must accommodate a large number of nodes. This chapter will teach you how to bring order back to such complex code bases. In this chapter, we will cover the following topics:

- Understanding the need for separate data storage
- Building hierarchical data structures
- Fetching data from classes
- Debugging data lookups
- Managing resources from data
- Data in modules and environments

Understanding the need for separate data storage

Looking back at what you have implemented during this book so far, you have managed to create some very versatile code that did very useful things in an automatic fashion. Your nodes can distribute entries for /etc/hosts among themselves. They register each other's public SSH key for authentication. A node can automatically register itself to a central Cacti server.

Thanks to Facter, Puppet has the information that allows the effortless handling of these use cases. Many configuration items are unique to each node only because they refer to a detail (such as an IP address or a generated key) that is already defined. Sometimes, the required configuration data can only be found on a remote machine, which Puppet handles through exported resources. Such manifest designs that can rely on facts are very economical. The information has already been gathered, and a single class can most likely behave correctly for many or all of your nodes, and can manage a common task in a graceful manner.

However, some configuration tasks have to be performed individually for each node, and these can incorporate settings that are rather arbitrary and not directly derived from the node's existing properties:

- In a complex MySQL replication setup that spans multiple servers, each participant requires a unique server ID. Duplicates must be prevented under any circumstances, so randomly generating the ID numbers is not safe
- Some of your networks might require regular maintenance jobs to be run from cron. Puppet should define a starting time for each machine to prevent the overlapping of the runs on any two machines
- In server operations, you have to perform the monitoring of the disk space usage on all systems. Most disks should generate early warnings so that there is time to react. However, other disks will be expected to be almost full most of the time, and should have a much higher warning threshold

When custom-built systems and software are managed through Puppet, they are also likely to require this type of micromanagement for each instance. The examples here represent only a tiny slice of the things that Puppet must manage explicitly and independently.

Consequences of defining data in the manifest

There are a number of ways in which a Puppet manifest can approach this problem of micromanagement. The most direct way is to define whole sets of classes one for each individual node:

```
class site::mysql_server01 {
  class { 'mysql': server_id => '1', ... }
}
class site::mysql_server02 {
  class { 'mysql': server_id => '2', ... }
}
...
class site::mysql_aux01 {
  class { 'mysql': server_id => '101', ... }
}
# and so forth ...
```

This is a very high-maintenance solution for the following reasons:

- The individual classes can become quite elaborate because all required `mysql` class parameters have to be used in each one
- There is much redundancy among the parameters that are, in fact, identical across all nodes
- The individually different values can be hard to spot, and must be carefully kept unique throughout the whole collection of classes
- This is only really feasible by keeping these classes close together, which might conflict with other organizational principles of your code base

In short, this is a brute-force approach that introduces its own share of cost. A more economic approach would be to pass the values that are different among nodes (and only those!) to a wrapper class:

```
node 'xndp12-sql09.example.net' {
  class { 'site::mysql_server':
    mysql_server_id => '103',
  }
}
```

This wrapper can declare the `mysql` class in a generic fashion, thanks to the individual parameter value per node:

```
class site::mysql_server(
  String $mysql_server_id
) {
  class { 'mysql':
    server_id => $mysql_server_id,
    ...
  }
}
```

This is much better because it eliminates the redundancy and its impact on maintainability. The wrinkle is that the `node` blocks can become quite messy with parameter assignments for many different subsystems. Explanatory comments contribute to the wall of text that each `node` block can become.

You can take this a step further by defining lookup tables in hash variables, outside of any `node` or `class`, on the global scope:

```
$mysql_config_table = {
  'xndp12-sql01.example.net' => {
    server_id   => '1',
    buffer_pool => '12G',
  },
  ...
}
```

This alleviates the need to declare any variables in `node` blocks. The classes look up the values directly from the hash:

```
class site::mysql_server(
  $config = $mysql_config_table[$::certname]
) {
  class { 'mysql':
    server_id => $config['server_id'],
    ...
  }
}
```

This is pretty sophisticated, and is actually close to the even better way that you will learn about later in this chapter. Note that this approach still retains a leftover possibility of redundancy. Some configuration values are likely to be identical among all nodes that belong to one group, but are unique to each group (for example, preshared keys of any variety).

This requires that all servers in the hypothetical `xndp12` cluster contain some key-value pairs that are identical for all members:

```
$crypt_key_xndp12 = 'xneFGl%23ndfAWLN34a0t9w30.zges4'
$config = {
'xndp12-stor01.example.net' => { $crypt_key =>
  $crypt_key_xndp12, ... },
'xndp12-stor02.example.net' => { $crypt_key =>
  $crypt_key_xndp12, ... },
 'xndp12-sql01.example.net' => { $crypt_key =>
  $crypt_key_xndp12, ... },
...
}
```

This is not ideal, but let's stop here. There is no point in worrying about even more elaborate ways to sort configuration data into recursive hash structures. Such solutions will quickly grow very difficult to understand and maintain anyway. The silver bullet is an external database that holds all individual and shared values. Before I go into the details of using Hiera for just this purpose, let's discuss the general ideas of hierarchical data storage.

Building hierarchical data structures

In the previous section, we reduced the data problem to a simple need for key-value pairs that are specific to each node under Puppet management. Puppet and its manifests then serve as the engine that generates actual configuration from these minimalistic bits of information.

A simplistic approach to this problem is an `ini` style configuration file that has a section for each node that sets values for all configurable keys. Shared values will be declared in one or more general sections:

```
[mysql]
buffer_pool=15G
log_file_size=500M
...
[xndp12-sql01.example.net]
psk=xneFGl%23ndfAWLN34a0t9w30.zges4
server_id=1
```

Rails applications customarily do something similar and store their configuration in a YAML format. The user can define different environments, such as `production`, `staging`, and `testing`. The values that are defined per environment override the global setting values.

This is quite close to the type of hierarchical configuration that Puppet allows through its Hiera binding. The hierarchies that the aforementioned Rails applications and `ini` files achieve through configuration environments are quite flat there is a global layer and an overlay for specialized configuration. With Hiera and Puppet, a single configuration database will typically handle whole clusters of machines and entire networks of such clusters. This implies the need for a more elaborate hierarchy.

Hiera allows you to define your own hierarchical layers. There are some typical, proven examples, which are found in many configurations out there:

- The `common` layer holds default values for all agents
- A `location` layer can override some values in accordance with the data center that houses each respective node
- Each agent machine typically fills a distinct `role` in your infrastructure, such as `wordpress_appserver` or `puppetdb_server`
- Some configurations are specific to each single `machine`

For example, consider the configuration of a hypothetical reporting client. Your `common` layer will hold lots of presets, such as default verbosity settings, the transport compression option, and other choices that should work for most machines. On the `location` layer, you ensure that each machine checks in to the respective local server reporting should not use WAN resources.

Settings per role are perhaps the most interesting part. They allow fine-grained settings that are specific to a class of servers. Perhaps your application servers should monitor their memory consumption in very close intervals. For the database servers, you will want a closer view of hard drive operations and performance. For your Puppet servers, there might be special plugins that gather specific data.

The `machine` layer is very useful in declaring any exceptions to the rule. There are always some machines that require special treatment for one reason or another. With a top hierarchy layer that holds data for each single agent, you get full control over all the data that an agent uses.

These ideas are still quite abstract, so let's finally look at the actual application of Hiera.

Configuring Hiera

The support for retrieving data values from Hiera has been built into Puppet since version 3. All you need in order to get started is a `hiera.yaml` file in the configuration directory.

Of course, the location and name of the configuration is customizable, as is almost everything that is related to configuration. Look for the `hiera_config` setting.

As the filename extension suggests, the configuration is in the YAML format and contains a hash with keys for the backends, the hierarchy, and backend-specific settings. The keys are noted as Ruby symbols with a leading colon:

```
# /etc/puppetlabs/puppet/hiera.yaml
:backends:
  - yaml
:hierarchy:
  - node/%{::clientcert}
  - role/%{::role}
  - location/%{::datacenter}
  - common
:yaml:
  :datadir: /etc/puppetlabs/code/environments/%{::environment}/hieradata
```

Note that the value of `:backends` is actually a single-element array. You can pick multiple backends. The significance will be explained later. The `:hierarchy` value contains a list of the actual layers that were described earlier. Each entry is the name of a data source. When Hiera retrieves a value, it searches each data source in turn. The `%{}` expression allows you to access the values of Puppet variables. Use only facts or global scope variables here; anything else will make Hiera's behavior quite confusing.

Finally, you will need to include configurations for each of your backends. The preceding configuration uses the YAML backend only, so there is only a hash for `:yaml` with the one supported `:datadir` key. This is where Hiera will expect to find YAML files with data. For each data source, the `datadir` can contain one `.yaml` file. As the names of the sources are dynamic, you will typically create more than four or five data source files. Let's create some examples before we have a short discussion on the combination of multiple backends.

Hiera version 5 was released with Puppet 4.9. This new version of Hiera uses another layout of the configuration file and offers more flexibility. We will first introduce Hiera 3, prior to explaining the setup, migration, and additional features of Hiera 5, as most of the basic concepts are identical.

Storing Hiera data

The backend of your Hiera setup determines how you have to store your configuration values. For the YAML backend, you fill `datadir` with files that each hold a hash of values. Let's put some elements of the reporting engine configuration into the example hierarchy:

```
# /etc/puppetlabs/code/environments/production/hieradata/common.yaml
reporting::server: stats01.example.net
reporting::server_port: 9033
```

The values in `common.yaml` are defaults that are used for all agents. They are at the broad base of the hierarchy. Values that are specific to a `location` or `role` apply to smaller groups of your agents. For example, the database servers of the `postgres` role should run some special reporting plugins:

```
# /etc/puppetlabs/code/environments/production/hieradata/role/postgres.yaml
reporting::plugins:
  - iops
  - cpuload
```

On such a high layer, you can also override the values from the lower layers. For example, a role-specific data source, such as `role/postgres.yaml`, can set a value for `reporting::server_port` as well. The layers are searched from the most to the least specific, and the first value is used. This is why it is a good idea to have a node-specific data source at the top of the hierarchy. On this layer, you can override any value for each agent. In this example, the reporting node can use the loopback interface to reach itself:

```
#/etc/puppetlabs/.../hieradata/node/stats01.example.net.yaml
reporting::server: localhost
```

Each agent receives a patchwork of configuration values according to the concrete YAML files that make up its specific hierarchy.

Don't worry if all this feels a bit overwhelming; there are more examples in this chapter. Hiera also has the charming characteristic of seeming rather complicated on paper, but it feels very natural and intuitive once you try using it yourself.

Choosing your backends

There are two built-in backends: YAML and JSON. This chapter will focus on YAML, because it's a very convenient and efficient form of data notation. The JSON backend is very similar to YAML. It looks for data in `.json` files instead of `.yaml` for each data source; these files use a different data notation format.

The use of multiple backends should never be truly necessary. In most cases, a well thought-out hierarchy will suffice for your needs. With a second backend, data lookup will traverse your hierarchy once per backend. This means that the lowest level of your primary backend will rank higher than any layer from additional backends.

In some cases, it might be worthwhile to add another backend just to get the ability to define even more basic defaults in an alternative location perhaps a distributed filesystem or a source control repository with different commit privileges.

Also, note that you can add custom backends to Hiera, so these might also be sensible choices for secondary or even tertiary backends. A Hiera backend is written in Ruby, like the Puppet plugins. The details of creating such a backend are beyond the scope of this book.

A particularly popular backend plugin is `eyaml`, available through the `hiera-eyaml` Ruby gem. This backend allows you to incorporate encrypted strings in your YAML data. Puppet decrypts the data upon retrieval.

> With Puppet 5, the eyaml plugin is already part of the Puppet build OS packages.

You have studied the theory of storing data in Hiera at length, so it's finally time to see how to make use of this in Puppet.

Fetching data from classes

Looking up a key value in Hiera is easy. Puppet comes with a very straightforward function for this:

```
$plugins = hiera('reporting::plugins')
```

Whenever the compiler encounters such a call in the manifest of the current agent node, it triggers a search in the hierarchy. The specific data sources are determined by the hierarchy in your `hiera.yaml` file. It will almost always rely on fact values provided by the agent to make flexible data source selections.

If the named key cannot be found in the agent's hierarchy, the master aborts the catalog compilation with an error. To prevent this, it is often sensible to supply a default value with the lookup:

```
$plugins = hiera('reporting::plugins', [])
```

In this case, Puppet uses an empty array if the hierarchy mentions no plugins.

On the other hand, you can purposefully omit the default value. Just as with `class` and `define` parameters, this signals that the Hiera value is required. If the user fails to supply it, Puppet will abort the manifest compilation.

Working with simple values

You have seen how to invoke the `hiera` function for value retrieval. There is really not more to it than what you have seen in the previous section, except for an optional parameter. It allows you to include an additional layer at the top of your hierarchy. If the key is found in the named data source, it will override the result from the regular hierarchy:

```
$plugins = hiera('reporting::plugins', [], 'global-overrides')
```

If the `reporting::plugins` key is found in the `global-overrides` data source, the value is taken from there. Otherwise, the normal hierarchy is searched.

Generally, assigning the retrieved value to a manifest variable is quite common. However, you can also invoke the `hiera` function in other useful contexts, such as the following:

```
@@cacti_device { $::fqdn:
  ip => hiera('snmp_address', $::ipaddress),
}
```

The lookup result can be handed to a resource directly as a parameter value. This is an example of how to allow Hiera to define a specific IP address per machine that should be used for a specific service. It acts as a simple way to manually override Facter's assumptions.

It is generally safer to store Hiera lookup results in a variable first. This allows you to check their data type. In Puppet 3, you need to use an `assert` function from the `stdlib` module. Puppet 4 has an operator for this purpose:

```
$max_threads = hiera('max_threads')
if $max_threads !~ Integer {
    fail "The max_threads value must be an integer number"
}
```

Another frequent occurrence is a parameter default that is made dynamic through a Hiera lookup:

```
define logrotate::config(
  Integer $rotations = hiera('logrotate::rotations', 7)
) {
  # regular define code here
}
```

For `logrotate::config` resources that are declared with an explicit parameter value, the Hiera value is ignored:

```
logrotate::config { '/var/log/cacti.log': rotations => 12 }
```

This can be a little confusing. Still, the pattern adds some convenience. Most agents can rely on the default. The hierarchy allows you to tune this default on multiple levels of granularity.

Binding class parameter values automatically

The concept of parameterized classes might have gotten a somewhat tarnished reputation, judging from our coverage of it so far. It allegedly makes it difficult to include classes from multiple places in the manifest, or silently allows it under shifting circumstances. While that is true, you can avoid these issues by relying on Hiera for your class parameterization needs.

Since Puppet's version 3.2, it has been possible to choose the values for any class's parameters right in the Hiera data. Whenever you include a class that has any parameters, Puppet will query Hiera to find a value for each of them. The keys must be named after the class and parameter names, joined by a double colon. Remember the cacti class from Chapter 5, *Combining Classes, Configuration Files, and Extensions into Modules*. It had a $redirect parameter. To define its value in Hiera, add the cacti::redirect key:

```
# node/cacti01.example.net.yaml
cacti::redirect: false
```

Some classes have very elaborate interfaces the apache class from the Puppet Labs Apache module accepts 70 parameters at the time of writing this. If you need many of those, you can put them into the target machine's dedicated YAML file as one coherent block of keys with values. It will be quite readable because the apache:: prefixes line up.

You don't save any lines compared to specifying the parameters right in the manifest, but at least the wall of options will not get in your way while you're programming in your manifests, you separated data from code.

The point that is perhaps the most redeeming for class parameterization is that each key is independent in your hierarchy. Many parameters can most likely be defined for many or all of your machines. Clusters of application servers can share some settings (if your hierarchy includes a layer on which they are grouped together), and you can override parameters for single machines as you see fit:

```
# common.yaml
apache::default_ssl_cert:
/etc/puppetlabs/puppet/ssl/certs/%{::clientcert}.pem
apache::default_ssl_key:
/etc/puppetlabs/puppet/ssl/private_keys/%{::clientcert}.pem
apache::purge_configs: false
```

The preceding example prepares your site to use the Puppet certificates for HTTPS. This is a good choice for internal services, because trust to the Puppet CA can be easily established, and the certificates are available on all agent machines. The third parameter, `purge_configs`, prevents the module from obliterating any existing Apache configuration that is not under Puppet's management.

Let's see an example of a more specific hierarchy layer that overrides this setting:

```
# role/httpsec.yaml
apache::purge_configs: true
apache::server_tokens: Minimal
apache::server_signature: off
apache::trace_enable: off
```

On machines that have the `httpsec` role, the Apache configuration should be purged so that it matches the managed configuration completely. The hierarchy of such machines also defines some additional values that are not defined in the `common` layer. The SSL settings from `common` remain untouched.

A specific machine's YAML can override keys from either layer if need be:

```
# node/sec02-sxf12.yaml
apache::default_ssl_cert: /opt/ssl/custom.pem
apache::default_ssl_key: /opt/ssl/custom.key
apache::trace_enable: extended
```

All these settings require no additional work. They take effect automatically, provided that the `apache` class from the `puppetlabs-apache` module is included.

For some users, this might be the only way in which Hiera is employed on their master, which is perfectly valid. You can even design your manifests specifically to expose all configurable items as class parameters. However, keep in mind that another advantage of Hiera is that any value can be retrieved from many different places in your manifest.

For example, if your firewalled servers are reachable through dedicated NAT ports, you will want to add those ports to each machine's Hiera data. The manifest can export this value not only to the firewall server itself, but also to external servers that use it in scripts and configurations to reach the exporting machine:

```
$nat_port = hiera('site::net::nat_port')
@@firewall { "650 forward port ${nat_port} to ${::fqdn}":
  proto       => 'tcp',
  dport       => $nat_port,
  destination => hiera('site::net::nat_ip'),
  jump        => 'DNAT',
  todest      => $::ipaddress,
```

```
    tag           => hiera('site::net::firewall_segment'),
}
```

The values will most likely be defined on different hierarchical layers. `nat_port` is agent-specific and can only be defined in the `%{::fqdn}` (or `%{::clientcert}` for better security) derived data source. `nat_ip` will probably be identical for all servers in the same cluster. They might share a server role. `firewall_segment` could well be identical for all servers that share the same location:

```
# stor03.example.net.yaml
site::net::nat_port: 12020
...
# role/storage.yaml
site::net::nat_ip: 198.58.119.126
...
# location/portland.yaml
site::net::firewall_segment: segment04
...
```

As previously mentioned, some of this data will be helpful in other contexts as well. Assume that you deploy a script through a defined type. The script sends messages to remote machines. The destination address and port are passed to the defined type as parameters. Each node that should be targeted can export this script resource:

```
@@site::maintenance_script {"/usr/local/bin/maint-${::fqdn}":
  address => hiera('site::net::nat_ip'),
  port    => hiera('site::net::nat_port'),
}
```

It would be impractical to do all this in one class that takes the port and address as parameters. You would want to retrieve the same value from within different classes or even modules, each taking care of the respective exports.

Handling hashes and arrays

Some examples in this chapter defined array values in Hiera. The good news is that retrieving arrays and hashes from Hiera is not at all different from retrieving simple strings, numbers, or Boolean values. The `hiera` function will return all these values, which are ready for use in the manifest.

There are two more functions that offer special handling for such values; the `hiera_array` and `hiera_hash` functions.

The presence of these functions can be somewhat confusing. New users might assume that these are required whenever retrieving hashes or arrays from the hierarchy. When inheriting Puppet code, it can be a good idea to double-check that these derived functions are actually used correctly in a given context.

When the `hiera_array` function is invoked, it gathers all named values from the whole hierarchy and merges them into one long array that comprises all elements that were found. Take the example of the distributed firewall configuration once more. Each node should be able to export a list of rules that open ports for public access. The manifest for this would be completely driven by Hiera:

```
if hiera('site::net::nat_ip', false) {
  @@firewall { "200 NAT ports for ${::fqdn}":
    port        => hiera_array('site::net::nat_ports'),
    proto       => 'tcp',
    destination => hiera('site::net::nat_ip'),
    jump        => 'DNAT',
    todest      => $::ipaddress,
  }
}
```

Please note that the title `200 NAT ports` does not allude to the number of ports, but just adheres to the naming conventions for `firewall` resources. The numeric prefix makes it easy to maintain order. Also, note the seemingly nonsensical default value of `false` for the `site::net::nat_ip` key in the `if` clause. This forms a useful pattern, though the resource should only be exported if `public_ip` is defined for the respective node.

Care must be taken if `false` or the empty string is a conceivable value for the key in question. In this case, the `if` clause will ignore that value. In such cases, you should use a well-defined comparison instead:

```
if hiera('feature_flag_A', undef) != undef { ... }
```

The hierarchy can then hold ports on several layers:

```
# common.yaml
nat_ports: 22
```

The SSH port should be available for all nodes that get a public address. Note that this value is not an array itself. This is fine Hiera will include scalar values in the resulting list without any complaints:

```
# role-webserver.yaml
nat_ports: [ 80, 443 ]
```

Standalone web application servers present their HTTP and HTTPS ports to the public:

```
# tbt-backend-test.example.net.yaml
nat_ports:
  - 5973
  - 5974
  - 5975
  - 6630
```

The testing instance for your new cloud service should expose a range of ports for custom services. If it has the `webserver` role (somehow), it will lead to an export of ports 22, 80, and 443, as well as its individually chosen list.

When designing such a construct, keep in mind that the array merge is only ever cumulative. There is no way to exclude values that were added in lower layers from the final result. In this example, you will have no opportunity to disable the SSH port 22 for any given machine. You should take good care when adding common values.

A similar alternative lookup function exists for hashes. The `hiera_hash` function also traverses the whole hierarchy and constructs a hash by merging all hashes it finds under the given Hiera key from all hierarchy layers. Hash keys in higher layers overwrite those from lower layers. All values must be hashes. Strings, arrays, or other data types are not allowed in this case:

```
# common.yaml
haproxy_settings:
  log_socket: /dev/log
  log_level: info
  user: haproxy
  group: haproxy
  daemon: true
```

These are the default settings for `haproxy` at the lowest hierarchy level. On web servers, the daemon should run as the general web service user:

```
# role/webserver.yaml
haproxy_settings:
  user: www-data
  group: www-data
```

When retrieved using `hiera('haproxy_settings')`, this will just evaluate to the hash, `{'user'=>'www-data', 'group'=>'www-data'}`. The hash at the role-specific layer completely overrides the default settings.

To get all values, create a merger using `hiera_hash('haproxy_settings')` instead. The result is likely to be more useful:

```
{ 'log_socket' =>'/dev/log', 'log_level' => 'info',
'user' => 'www-data', 'group' => 'www-data', 'daemon' => true }
```

The limitations are similar to those of `hiera_array`. Keys from any hierarchy level cannot be removed; they can only be overwritten with different values. The end result is quite similar to what you would get from replacing the hash with a group of keys:

```
# role/webserver.yaml
haproxy::user: www-data
haproxy::group: www-data
```

If you opt to do this, the data can also be easily fitted to a class that can bind these values to parameters automatically. Preferring flat structures can, therefore, be beneficial. Defining hashes in Hiera is still generally worthwhile, as the next section explains. `https://docs.puppetlabs.com/references/latest/function.html#createresou rces` originally been conceived for. Hiera can serve as a basic ENC.

Choosing between manifest and Hiera designs

You can now move most of the concrete configuration to the data storage.
Classes can be included from the manifest or through Hiera. Puppet looks up parameter values in the hierarchy, and you can flexibly distribute the configuration values there in order to achieve the desired result for each node with minimal effort and redundancy.

This does not mean that you don't write actual manifest code anymore. The manifest is still the central pillar of your design. You will often need logic that uses the configuration data as input. For example, there might be classes that should only be included if a certain value is retrieved from Hiera:

```
if hiera('use_caching_proxy', false) {
    include nginx
}
```

If you try and rely on Hiera exclusively, you will have to add `nginx` to the `classes` array at all places in the hierarchy that set the `use_caching_proxy` flag to `true`. This is prone to mistakes. What's worse is that the flag can be overridden from `true` to `false` at a more specific layer, but the `nginx` element cannot be removed from an array that is retrieved by `hiera_include`.

It is important to keep in mind that the manifest and data should complement each other. You should primarily build manifests and add lookup function calls at opportune places. Defining flags and values in Hiera should allow you (or the user of your modules) to alter the behavior of the manifest. The data should not be the driver of the catalog composition, except for places in which you replace large numbers of static resources with large data structures.

Debugging data lookups

As you can see from the preceding example, the data that contributes to the complete configuration of any module can be rather dispersed throughout the set of your data sources. It can be challenging to determine where the respective values are retrieved from for any given agent node. It can be frustrating to trace data sources to find out why a change at some level will not take effect for some of your agents.

To help make the process more transparent, Hiera comes with a command-line tool called `hiera`. Invoking it is simple:

```
root@puppetmaster # hiera -c /etc/puppetlabs/code/hiera.yaml demo::atoms
```

It retrieves a given key using the specified configuration from `hiera.yaml`. Make sure that you use the same Hiera configuration as Puppet.

Of course, this can only work sensibly if Hiera selects the same data sources as the compiler, which uses fact values to form a concrete hierarchy. These required facts can be given right on the command line as the final parameters:

```
root@puppetmaster # hiera -c /etc/puppetlabs/code/hiera.yaml demo::atoms
::clientcert=int01-web01.example.net ::role=webserver ::location=ny
```

This prints the `demo::atoms` value of the specified server to the console. The fact values can also be retrieved from a YAML file or other alternative sources. Use `hiera --help` to get information about the available scenarios.

Make sure that you add the `-d` (or `--debug`) flag in order to get helpful information about the traversal of the hierarchy:

```
root@puppetmaster # hiera -d -c ...
```

Hiera 5 allows for another way of debugging data lookups. We will cover
Hiera 5 later in this chapter.

Managing resources from data

You can now move configuration settings to Hiera and dedicate your manifest to logic. This
works seamlessly as far as classes and their parameters are concerned, because class
parameters automatically retrieve their values from Hiera. For configuration that requires
you to instantiate resources, you still need to write the full manifests and add manual
lookup function calls.

For example, an Apache web server requires some global settings, but the interesting parts
of its configuration are typically performed in virtual host configuration files. Puppet
models them with defined resource types. If you want to configure an `iptables` firewall,
you have to declare lots of resources of the `firewall` type (available through the
`puppetlabs-firewall` module).

Such elaborate resources can clutter up your manifest, yet they mostly represent data. There
is no inherent logic to many firewall rules (although sometimes a set of rules is derived
from one or several key values). Virtual hosts often stand for themselves as well, with little
or no relation to configuration details that are relevant to other parts of the setup.

Puppet comes with yet another function that allows you to move whole sets of such
resources to Hiera data. The pattern is straightforward: a group of resources of the same
type are represented by a hash. The keys are resource titles, and the values are yet another
layer of hashes with key-value pairs for attributes:

```
services:
  apache2:
    enable: true
    ensure: running
  syslog-ng:
    enable: false
```

This YAML data represents two `service` resources. To make Puppet add them as actual resources to the catalog, use the iterator function from Puppet 4:

```
$resource_hash.each |$res_title,$attributes| {
  service { $res_title:
    ensure => $attributes['ensure'],
    enable => $attributes['enable'],
  }
}
```

Within older Puppet code, one will most likely find the usage of the `create_resources` function:

```
$resource_hash = hiera('services', {})
create_resources('service', $resource_hash)
```

The first argument is the name of the resource type, and the second must be the hash of actual resources. There are some more aspects to this technique, but do note that, with Puppet 4, it is no longer necessary to rely on the `create_resources` function.

It's useful to be aware of the basics of it anyway. It is still in broad use for existing manifests, and it is still the most compact way of converting data into resources. To learn more, refer to the online documentation at `https://docs.puppetlabs.com/references/latest/function.html#createresources`.

The Puppet 4 iterator has a few advantages over the `create_resources` approach:

- You can perform data transformations, such as adding a prefix to string values, or deriving additional attribute values
- Each iteration can do more than just creating one resource per inner hash, for example, including required classes
- You can devise a data structure that deviates from the strict expectancies of `create_resources`
- The manifest is more clear and intuitive, especially to uninitiated readers

For creating many simple resources (such as the services in the preceding example), you might wish to avoid `create_resource` in Puppet 4 manifests. Just keep in mind that if you don't take advantage of doing so, you can keep the manifest more succinct by sticking to `create_resources` after all.

Puppet 4 comes with a useful tool to generate YAML data that is suitable for `create_resources`. With the following command, you can make Puppet emit service type resources that represent the set of available services on the local system, along with their current property values:

```
puppet resource -y service
```

The `-y` switch selects a YAML output instead of Puppet DSL.

In theory, these techniques allow you to move almost all your code to Hiera data (the next section discusses how desirable that really is). There is one more feature that goes one step further in this direction:

```
hiera_include('classes')
```

This call gathers values from all over the hierarchy; just the same as `hiera_array`. The resulting array is interpreted as a list of class names. All these named classes are included. This allows for some additional consolidation in your manifest:

```
# common.yaml
classes:
  - ssh
  - syslog
...
# role-webserver.yaml
classes:
  - apache
  - logrotate
  - syslog
```

You can possibly even use `hiera_include` to declare these classes outside of any `node` block. The data will then affect all nodes. Additionally, from some distinct classes, you might also declare other classes via `hiera_include`, whose names are stored under a different Hiera key.

The ability to enumerate classes for each node to include is what Puppet's **External Node Classifiers** (**ENCs**) had originally been conceived for. Hiera can serve as a basic ENC thanks to the `hiera_include` function. This is most likely preferred over writing a custom ENC. However, it should be noted that some open source ENCs, such as Foreman, are quite powerful and can add much more convenience; as a result, Hiera has not supplanted the concept as a whole.

The combination of these tools opens some ways for you to shrink your manifests to their essential parts and configure your machines gracefully through Hiera.

Hiera version 5

Hiera 5 was released with Puppet 4.9. Earlier Puppet 4 releases had Hiera 4 bundled. The main difference between older Hiera and Hiera 5 is the concept of multilayered Hiera hierarchies:

- The first layer is the module layer. Hiera 5 allows you to use Hiera data in modules by specifying a Hiera 5 config version `hiera.yaml` file inside the module root
- The second layer is the environment layer where you place a `hiera.yaml` file inside the environment root

The last layer is the main layer, where `hiera.yaml` resides in `/etc/puppetlabs/puppet/hiera.yaml`. This was the only layer available in older Hiera versions.

> The main layer is no longer considered best practice, and exists for compatibility reasons. Everybody is encouraged to migrate data from the main layer to the environment layer.

With Hiera 5, the configuration file has completely different content. It is still a YAML style file, but backends are no longer globally configured but put into the hierarchy level. This allows you to specify different backends for different Hiera hierarchies.

Let's convert the `hiera.yaml` file from Hiera 3 to Hiera 5:

```
# /etc/puppetlabs/puppet/hiera.yaml
:backends:
  - yaml
:hierarchy:
  - node/%{::clientcert}
  - role/%{::role}
  - location/%{::datacenter}
  - common
:yaml:
  :datadir: /etc/puppetlabs/code/environments/%{::environment
    }/hieradata
```

Transform this file to the Hiera 5 `.yaml` file:

```
# /etc/puppetlabs/code/environments/production/hiera.yaml
---
version: 5
# specify the default datadir and yaml backend
defaults:
  datadir: hieradata
  data_hash: yaml_data
# build hierarchy. Note that paths need the file ending!
hierarchy:
  - name: "Per-node data"
    path: "node/%{::clientcert}.yaml"
  - name: "Per-role data"
    path: "role/%{::role}.yaml"
  - name: "Per-location data"
    path: "location/%{::datacenter}.yaml"
  - name: "Common data"
    path: 'common.yaml'
```

Besides this, it is possible to configure the Hiera lookup behavior by adding `lookup_options` keys to your Hiera data. On each data lookup, Hiera 5 will first check for the `lookup_options` key and will then use this information to look up the desired data. But how should Hiera know which layer to use?

With Hiera 3 we used the `hiera`, `hiera_array`, or `hiera_hash` function to retrieve data. With Hiera 5, these functions have been replaced by a single lookup function.

- `hiera` (key) gets converted to lookup(key)
- `hiera_array` (key) gets converted to lookup(key, array, unique)
- `hiera_hash` (key) gets converted to lookup(key, hash, hash)

The automatic data lookup from classes works without any further changes. Another change with Hiera 5 is the way we debug Hiera data lookups. Puppet now has the puppet lookup interface. Remember the Hiera cli tool:

```
root@puppetmaster # hiera -c /etc/puppetlabs/code/hiera.yaml demo::atoms
::clientcert=int01-web01.example.net ::role=webserver ::location=ny
```

Now we can use the Puppet lookup cli:

```
root@puppetmaster
# puppet lookup demo::atoms -node int01-web01.example.net
```

The main difference is that Puppet lookup uses facts stored on the Puppet master instead of adding each used fact on cli. Besides this, there is an additional option --explain, which replaces the debug option from Hiera cli.

When using Puppet lookup with the --explain option, the output also shows the lookup for the merge behavior.

Describing all of the new features, especially the paths and globbing possibilities and the configuration of Hiera lookup behavior inside Hiera, is beyond the scope of this book:

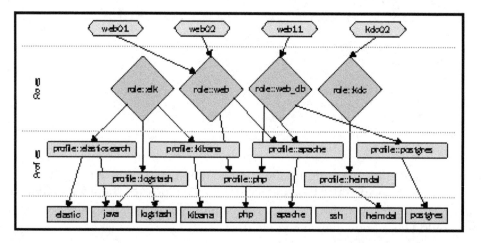

http://www.craigdunn.org/2012/05/239/, and the design has since been adopted by many users.

Summary

Hiera is a tool that stores and retrieves data in a hierarchical fashion. Each retrieval uses a distinct data source from each hierarchy layer and traverses your hierarchy from the most to the least specific level. The hierarchy is defined by the user as an array in a YAML file.

Puppet has Hiera support built in, and you can use it to separate data from code. From manifests, you will mainly perform lookups through the `hiera` function. In most cases, the respective entries will rely on fact values.

Another common way to employ Hiera through Puppet is to name the Hiera keys in the `<class-name>::<parameter-name>` format. When including a parameterized class, Puppet will look for such keys in Hiera. If the manifest does not supply a parameter value, Puppet automatically binds the value from Hiera to the respective parameter.

Manifests that boast large numbers of static resources can be cleaned up by converting the declarations to hashes and using the `create_resources` or `each` function to declare resources from the data.

Hiera 5 offers a broad set of new functionality, including data in modules and data in environments. This chapter gave you guidance on how to migrate data to Hiera 5.

Within `Chapter 9`, *Puppet Roles and Profiles*, we will discuss how modules and node classification should work together, and how to automatically build and deploy a Puppet code environment.

9
Puppet Roles and Profiles

Now that we have a complete overview of the Puppet DSL and its concepts, it is time to look at how to build implementations based on Puppet that reflect your infrastructure settings and requirements.

In the early days of Puppet, it was common practice to add resources and variables to a node classification. This mostly led to duplicate code and made refactoring almost impossible. This pattern mostly reflected the usual admin work, which was done by configuring individual systems.

To avoid difficult to manage and hard to maintain code, a community around Puppet modules emerged. This community took care to implement technical parts of a system into Puppet modules. Modules have the benefit of being reusable by parameters and get bug-fixes and new implementations faster due to shared efforts.

As we now have a large set of modules available, we must rethink the pattern of our node classification in combination with modules. Here, the roles and profiles pattern comes into play.

Within this chapter, the following topics will be covered:

- Technical component modules
- Implementing components in profiles
- Building roles from profiles
- The business use case and the node classification
- Placing code on the Puppet server

Technical component modules

Until now, we have referred to modules as a strict directory structure containing classes, static files, templates, and extensions. We now must differentiate between upstream or generic modules and our platform implementation modules.

Modules that take care of a specific technical component are now referred to as technical component modules. Technical components themselves are a set of configurations for a certain software running on a system, such as Nginx, Postgres, or LDAP.

There has always been the problem of whether a module is a technical component module or not. There are some patterns that allow you to identify technical component modules:

- Developed upstream with active community
- Open source with README and LICENSE files
- Only manages what is required
- Clearly described entry class with parameters for adoption and reusability
- Allows stacking together with other technical component classes
- Uses a module name related to the configured technology
- Usually has support for multiple operating systems
- Has public information such as package and configuration filenames
- Does not have private data, as your internal DNS server IP

Implementing components in profiles

Puppet code that is not taken from upstream, but developed in-house describing your infrastructure, usually is an implementation of resources and upstream classes. This implementation is called a profile class.

Technically, a profile is a module containing classes, and optionally has parameters, defines, files, and templates. On very rare occasions, it might be valuable to also have custom facts or custom functions within profiles.

Inside a profile, one specifies data and resources. Data can either be static data, which is valid for the whole platform, or placed into Hiera. Resources can be anything such as class, file, package, and service.

Combining these into a profile builds another layer of abstraction:

- Data is abstracted by Hiera
- CLI commands are abstracted by resource types
- Resource types are abstracted by technical component modules
- Technical component modules are abstracted by profiles

 When one searches for profiles on the internet, you will mostly find stubs with Apache, MySQL, and WordPress installation.

Profiles are not meant to be made public, as they usually contain private information about your infrastructure. Instead, one has to develop profiles on their own.

Let's start with an example: a `phpmyadmin` based database management system.

The system consists of several base technical components: remote login, backup, firewall, webserver, database, `php`, and `phpmyadmin`. Each of these components is managed by an upstream developed technical component module. The way we want to have the implementation is done in profiles:

```
# Class profile::login
#
# manages ssh access
# company policy requires the following settings:
# - forbid root login
# - forbid x11 forwarding
# - allow login based on group (admins)
#
# We have several other settings which are put into our own
# sshd_config template file
#
class profile::login {
  class { 'ssh':
    sshd_x11_forwarding    => false,
    sshd_config_template   =>
    epp('profile/login/sshd_config.epp'),
    sshd_config_allowgroups => ['admins'],
    permit_root_login      => 'no',
  }
}
```

Instead of writing a single profile for every different setup, it is possible to either add parameters to the profile and make use of Hiera lookup, or to stack components together:

```
# Class profile::login::secure
#
# Reuses profile::login classes
# adds known_host_file based on template
#
class profile::login::secure {
  include profile::ssh
  file { '/etc/ssh/ssh_known_hosts':
    ensure  => file,
    content => epp('profile/login/ssh_known_hosts.epp'),
  }
}
```

The same pattern can be used for MySQL. The main `mysql` profile just installs a single MySQL instance using the `puppetlabs-mysql` module:

```
# Class profile::database::mysql
#
# Needs data in hiera:
# - mysql_root_password (String), defaults to 123456
# - mysql_database (Hash)
#
class profile::database::mysql {
  $mysql_root_password = lookup('mysql_root_password', String, 'first',
'123456')
  $mysql_database = lookup('mysql_database', Hash, 'deep', '')
  class { 'mysql':
    root_password           => $mysql_root_password,
    remove_default_accounts => true,
  }
  class { 'mysql::bindings':
    php_enable => true,
  }
  $mysql_database.each |$db, $options| {
    mysql::db { $db:
      * => $options,
    }
  }
}
```

The same pattern follows for the `php` and `phpmyadmin` installation using upstream modules:

```
# Class profile::scripting::php
#
# uses puppet/php mdoule
# basic installation only
#
class profile::scripting::php {
  include ::php
}
# Class profile::apps::phpmyadmin
#
# uses jlondon/phpmyadmin
# configures the application and application vhost
#
class profile::apps::phpmyadmin {
  class { 'phpmyadmin': }
  phpmyadmin::server{ 'default': }
  phpmyadmin::vhost { 'internal.domain.net':
    vhost_enabled => true,
    priority      => '20',
    docroot       => $phpmyadmin::params::doc_path,
    ssl           => true,
  }
}
# Class profile::apps::phpmyadmin::db
#
# uses jlondon/phpmyadmin module
# exports the setting for phpmyadmin
#
class profile::apps::phpmyadmin::db {
  @@phpmyadmin::servernode { "${::ipaddress}":
    server_group => 'default',
  }
}
```

Grouping profiles within a directory structure has no technical need. Think about an infrastructure that has lots of profiles or even lots of similar profiles, such as PostgreSQL, MySQL, MariaDB, Galera Cluster, or Oracle DB, and MSSQL. In this case, the grouping is preferred to flat file space, as many flat files lead to a difficult to read directory structure:

```
profile/
|- manifests/
|    |- apps/
|    |    |— phpmyadmin/
|    |    |    \- db.pp
```

```
|      |     \- phpmyadmin.pp
|      |- database/
|      |     \- mysql.pp
|      |- login/
|      |     \- secure.pp
|      |- login.pp
|      \- scripting/
|           \— php.pp
\- templates/
     \- login/
            |- sshd_config.epp
            \- ssh_known_hosts.epp
```

The business use case and node classification

With all implementations now being in place, we look forward to how to do node classification.

There are several options available and which one is the best solution mostly depends on your platform.

When you have a very diverse platform, the concept of roles as another abstraction layer is not very useful, as it mostly leads to duplicate code. In this case, most people decided to use profiles for node classification.

When you have large sets of identically configured systems, one wants to go ahead with the role pattern and classify systems by their business use case.

The business use case allows you to describe systems not by what they do, but by what they are used for.

Think about the `phpmyadmin` installation. Depending on use case and business owner, one might have different classification names:

A technician will use the term `database control panel`. If the `phpmyadmin` installation is used by the sales team, it might be possible that they name the same system `crm data management system`.

The best solution is to identify the application stake holder and ask what the application is used for. This has the positive side effect of getting an overview of all business use cases. If you identify a system having more than one business use case, it is now easy to understand the business impact in the event of a system outage.

In the past, people stacked many applications onto a single system to allow for the best hardware usage. These are infrastructures where one node will have multiple business use cases. With the concept of virtual machines, this is obsolete. Today, a single virtual machine should serve a single business use case only.

Building roles from profiles

Let's continue with the phpmyadmin example, which has been built for the sales department so that they can manage their CRM database.

In this case, we build a role for that system based on implementation profiles. The name of the role reflects the business use case:

```
class role::crm_db_control_panel {
  contain profile::login::secure
  contain profile::database::mysql
  contain profile::scripting::php
  contain profile::apps::phpmyadmin::db
  contain profile::apps::phpmyadmin
}
```

Within a role, one only declares profiles. No code logic, no resources, no data lookups. This allows flexible use of roles. Don't try to build almost identical roles, as this will lead to duplicate code. Instead, it would be better to create profiles with data lookups to reflect individual usage.

The previously mentioned role can then be used for a node classification:

```
node 'dbcrmmgmt.domain.com' {
  contain role::crm_db_control_panel
}
```

As you can now see, we have a single instance with a single role. This is always useful when building systems from scratch. Within existing infrastructures, one can use this concept to identify which business units are affected when a single system is not available. Besides this, one learns about where to separate services when required.

There are environments where the concept of roles and profiles does not fit very well. Mostly, these are existing platforms where multiple services (roles) are running on a single system and many different implementations for the same profile exist. In these cases, one should verify whether the implementation layer (profile) alone is sufficient.

Placing code on the Puppet server

From a technical perspective, roles and profiles are classes inside modules. Usually, modules are put into the `modules` directory of an environment. But roles and profiles are different to modules, as they are implementations of modules and collections of implementations.

To reflect this different behavior, it is common practice to add another `module` directory to an environment. This configuration can be done in the `environment.conf` file inside an environment:

```
#/etc/puppetlabs/code/environments/production/environment.conf
modulepath = site:modules:$basemodulepath
```

Within our example, we have added a new path to the module path setting: site. This directory resides inside our environment (`/etc/puppetlabs/code/environments/production/site`). This directory will have all of our roles and profiles:

```
/etc/puppetlabs/code/environment/production/site/
  |- profile/
  |  |- manifests/
  |  |  |- apps/
  |  |  |  |- phpmyadmin/
  |  |  |  |  \- db.pp
  |  |  |  \- phpmyadmin.pp
  |  |  |- database/
  |  |  |  \- mysql.pp
  |  |  |- login/
  |  |  |  \- secure.pp
  |  |  |- login.pp
  |  |  \ - scripting/
  |  |  \- php.pp
  |  \- templates/
  |  \- login/
  |  |- sshd_config.epp
  |  \- ssh_known_hosts.epp
```

```
\- role/
    \- manifests/
        \- db_control_panel.pp
```

This allows us to keep roles and profiles in a separate directory structure and have modules by itself.

The Puppet control repository

Usually, Puppet modules are the same as libraries that are developed upstream. We want to ensure that modules that we use within our Puppet code are stored in a way that allows upgrades. Therefore, we cannot place the modules directly in our environment Git repository. Besides this, we want to test Puppet code updates prior to putting them into production.

Best practice is to have a control repository that has our roles and profiles, the manifest's node classification, the environment configuration file, and Hiera v5 configuration. Now we add another file: Puppetfile.

A Puppetfile references modules and, optionally, their source location and version:

```
# Third Party modules
mod "puppetlabs/concat", '3.0.0' # postgresql requires concat < 3.0.0
mod "puppetlabs/stdlib", :latest
mod "puppetlabs/aws", :latest
mod "jdowning/rbenv", :latest
mod "puppet/archive", :latest
mod "puppetlabs/inifile", :latest
# Used by profile::puppet::server
mod 'puppetlabs/postgresql', :latest
mod 'puppetlabs/puppetdb', :latest
mod 'puppet/puppetserver',
  :git => "https://github.com/voxpupuli/puppet-puppetserver.git",
  :tag => '2.1.0'
mod 'puppetlabs/puppetserver_gem', :latest
mod 'puppet/r10k', :latest
# mod 'puppet/puppetboard', :latest
```

When no source is given, the module will be installed from Puppet Forge (https://forge.puppet.com). As most production systems are not allowed to connect to the internet, it is useful to have a clone of the upstream module development repository on your private Git server.

A Puppet control repository can have the following files and directory structure:

```
control-repo/
 |- environment.conf
 |- hieradata/
 |- hiera.yaml
 |- manifests/
 | |- dmz.pp
 | |- internal.pp
 | \- site.pp
 |- Puppetfile
 |- README.md
 \- site/
     |- profile/
     | |- manifests/
     | | |- apps/
     | | | |- phpmyadmin/
     | | | | \- db.pp
     | | | \- phpmyadmin.pp
     | | |- database/
     | | | \- mysql.pp
     | | |- login/
     | | | \- secure.pp
     | | |- login.pp
     | | \- scripting/
     | | \- php.pp
     | \- templates/
     | \- login/
     | |- sshd_config.epp
     | \- ssh_known_hosts.epp
     \- role/
         \- manifests/
             \- db_control_panel.pp
```

Synchronizing upstream modules

Usually, one can use the workstation for synchronization. First, an empty repository is created on the local Git server and cloned to the workstation. Within this local repository, a new remote location is added:

```
git remote add github https://github.com/puppetlabs/puppetlabs-concat.git
```

Now the upstream code is fetched:

```
$ git pull github master
remote: Counting objects: 2871, done.
remote: Compressing objects: 100% (11/11), done.
remote: Total 2871 (delta 1), reused 7 (delta 1), pack-reused 2859
Receiving objects: 100% (2871/2871), 634.98 KiB | 648.00 KiB/s, done.
Resolving deltas: 100% (1394/1394), done.
From https://github.com/puppetlabs/puppetlabs-concat
* branch master -> FETCH_HEAD
```

Git separates code and objects. Usually, upstream uses tags to identify version releases of their module. Tags are part of the non-code objects. Next, the non-code objects are fetched:

```
git fetch --all
Fetching origin
Fetching github
remote: Counting objects: 33, done.
remote: Compressing objects: 100% (29/29), done.
remote: Total 33 (delta 8), reused 28 (delta 3), pack-reused 0
Unpacking objects: 100% (33/33), done.
From https://github.com/puppetlabs/puppetlabs-concat
* [new branch] 1.0.x -> github/1.0.x
[...]
   * [new tag] 3.0.0 -> 3.0.0
   * [new tag] 4.0.0 -> 4.0.0
   * [new tag] 4.0.1 -> 4.0.1
```

Now the local repository server gets the code pushed:

```
$ git push origin master
   Counting objects: 2871, done.
Compressing objects: 100% (1368/1368), done.
    Writing objects: 100% (2871/2871), 634.76 KiB | 0 bytes/s, done.
Total 2871 (delta 1394), reused 2871 (delta 1394)
To /var/repositories/puppetlabs-concat.git
* [new branch] master -> master
```

Don't forget to also push the tags:

```
$ git push origin master --tags
Counting objects: 19, done.
Compressing objects: 100% (19/19), done.
Writing objects: 100% (19/19), 11.01 KiB | 0 bytes/s, done.
Total 19 (delta 0), reused 0 (delta 0)
To /var/repositories/puppetlabs-concat.git
 * [new tag] 0.1.0 -> 0.1.0
[...]
```

```
* [new tag]     3.0.0 -> 3.0.0
* [new tag]     4.0.0 -> 4.0.0
* [new tag]     4.0.1 -> 4.0.1
```

R10K code deployment

Usually, companies have staging systems where a new development is tested prior to being put into production. The development team has a development stage. From this stage, the changes will be deployed to a quality gate stage and placed into the production stage after successful tests.

Many people use these names for the Puppet code environments. But what happens if your Puppet change will break the whole development stage? In this case, the development team is unable to continue working on urgent improvements or fixes. This can lead to time and cost intensive work where the development stage is built from scratch.

But how do we develop and test Puppet code changes? Usually, this requires another stage for infrastructure developers. All other infrastructure stages (development, QA, production) are then deployed using the stable production Puppet environment code.

This leads to two Puppet environments: **development** and **production**.

But we don't want these to be two separate Git repositories, as this makes the staging of changes very difficult. This is where R10K comes into place. R10K uses branches on the Puppet control repository and deploys these onto the Puppet Master as environments. Code changes can now be done by merge requests from one branch to another.

Names of branches can be freely chosen, except some special names that should not be used: master, agent, main. Especially for Git repositories, where the default branch will be master, this needs some reconfiguration on the default branch name.

R10K must be installed and configured on the Puppet Master. We can use Puppet for installation:

```
$ puppet resource package r10k ensure=present provider=puppet_gem
package { 'r10k':
  ensure => ['2.5.5'],
}
```

The `r10k` configuration file must be placed at `/etc/puppetlabs/r10k/r10k.yaml`. Within this file, we activate the desired `cache` directory where `r10k` stores local copies of all repositories. Remember to keep these caches in clean state and remove the whole cache in a case of misbehavior relating to the local Git repository caches.

R10K allows the usage of multiple control-repositories. These can easily coexist within one environment, as they get prefixed with the source name provided. Control repositories are placed into the sources section and get a unique name. Then, we specify the remote URL where R10K can get the code from. Code is deployed into the path mentioned within the basedir setting.

The last two settings are related to fetching code. The first one refers to Git access. Within the Git setting, one can set a provider. There are two providers available: shellgit and rugged. The shellgit provider uses the git binary, which must be available on the Puppet master. The user who runs the R10K command must have a configured git shell environment, as specifying the ssh key to use for authorization. Rugged is a Ruby implementation where one can specify the Git ssh settings directly in a r10k.yaml file. Usually, shellgit is sufficient to use. The last setting specifies how R10K should fetch modules from Puppet Forge. Here, we can only specify a proxy that should be used:

```
# /etc/puppetlabs/r10k/r10k.yaml
---
 cachedir: '/var/cache/r10k'
   sources:
   infrastructure:
    remote: 'https://gitserver/infra/r10k-control-repo.git'
   basedir: '/etc/puppetlabs/code/environments'
   qa:
    remote: 'https://gitserver/security/r10k-control-repo.git'
   basedir: '/etc/puppetlabs/code/environments'
    prefix: true
git:
  provider: shellgit
     forge:
   # proxy: 'http://proxyserver:port'
```

The deployment of branches from a control repository and installation of modules is done by running r10k. Please ensure that you run this command only as the user who needs to fetch the code. When running this command as root, either ssh credentials might be wrong or the environment belongs to the root user afterwards. The parameter -v enables verbose mode:

```
# r10k deploy environment -v# r10k deploy environment -vINFO -> Deploying
environment /etc/puppetlabs/code/r10k/developmentINFO -> Environment
development is now at db43d907d5b39d6197e42fc5c8edb4c0a4db27d6[...]INFO ->
Deploying environment /etc/puppetlabs/code/r10k/productionINFO ->
Environment production is now at
149a903d027d69d88a50ef3a563cb432c1e087c4[...]INFO -> Deploying environment
/etc/puppetlabs/code/r10k/qa_developmentINFO -> Environment qa_development
is now at db43d907d5b39d6197e42fc5c8edb4c0a4db27d6[...]INFO -> Deploying
```

```
environment /etc/puppetlabs/code/r10k/qa_productionINFO -> Environment
production is now at 149a903d027d69d88a50ef3a563cb432c1e087c4
```

Instead of manually running the r10K command-line tool, it is possible to install a webhook using the puppet-r10k module from voxpupuli (https://github.com/voxpupili/puppet-r10k):

```
class profile::puppet::master::r10k_webhook {
  class {'r10k::webhook::config':
    enable_ssl      => false,
    use_mcollective => false,
  }
  class {'r10k::webhook':
    use_mcollective => false,
    user            => 'root',
    group           => '0',
  }
}
```

This webhook can be triggered from Git server or from a CI/CD test/deployment toolchain such as Jenkins or GoCD. Usually, a combination of both is a valid setup, where you want to deploy feature branches as fast as possible and run updates on a development or a production environment only after successful tests.

Summary

When building and maintaining Puppet code bases, it is a good idea to implement the roles and profiles pattern. It makes you define roles to cover all of your machine use cases. The roles mix and match profile classes, which are basically collectors of classes from custom and open source modules that manage actual resources.

When setting up your first large Puppet installation, it is a good idea to adhere to the pattern from day one, because it will allow you to scale your manifests without getting tangled up in complicated structures.

Deployment of Puppet code is managed via r10k, where Git branch names reflect your Puppet code quality. Using Puppetfile allows you to separate your own Puppet code development from upstream module development.

This concludes our tour of *Puppet Essentials*. We have covered quite some ground, but as you can imagine, we barely scratched the surface of some of the topics, such as Puppet code testing, provider development, or exploiting PuppetDB. What you have learned will most likely satisfy your immediate requirements. For information beyond these lessons, don't hesitate to look up the excellent online documentation at `https://docs.puppet.com/`, or join the community and ask your questions in chat, Slack, or on the mailing list.

Thanks for reading, and have lots of fun with Puppet and its family of management tools.

Index

CPSIA information can be obtained
at www.ICGtesting.com
Printed in the USA
LVHW01s2308210218
567519LV00003B/88/P

9 781787 284715